Timothy Sprigge was born in 1932. He graduated in English at Gonville and Caius College, Cambridge, transferring to Moral Sciences (Philosophy) for his Ph.D. Since 1979 he has been Professor of Logic and Metaphysics at the University of Edinburgh. Previously he taught philosophy for fifteen years at the University of Sussex. Before that he held a research post at University College, London, working on the Bentham manuscripts there. His other publications include *Correspondence of Jeremy Bentham* (ed.), Vols. 1 and 2 (1968), *Facts, Words and Beliefs* (1970), *Santayana: An Examination of His Philosophy* (1974), and *The Vindication of Absolute Idealism* (1983). He is presently working on the theory of universals, on non-human rights and on the philosophies of F. H. Bradley and William James.

T. L. S. SPRIGGE

THEORIES OF EXISTENCE

PENGUIN BOOKS

Penguin Books Ltd, Harmondsworth, Middlesex, England
Viking Penguin Inc., 40 West 23rd Street, New York, New York 10010, U.S.A.
Penguin Books Australia Ltd, Ringwood, Victoria, Australia
Penguin Books Canada Limited, 2801 John Street, Markham, Ontario, Canada L3R 1B4
Penguin Books (N.Z.) Ltd, 182–190 Wairau Road, Auckland 10, New Zealand

First published 1985
Reprinted 1986

Made and printed in Great Britain by
Richard Clay (The Chaucer Press) Ltd,
Bungay, Suffolk
Set in Monophoto Photina

FOR LUCY, NINA AND SAM

CONTENTS

PREFACE

This work offers accounts of a number of important 'theories of existence' which have been offered by philosophers in the course of the last few centuries. By a theory of existence I understand a general view about the nature of reality and in particular about the nature of a human individual and his place in reality as a whole, a view which influences the whole way in which one who adopts it views the human situation and its problems and opportunities.

Theories of existence have been developed by thinkers who were not philosophers in any specialist sense. In this book, however, I am solely concerned with the theories of existence which have been put forward by philosophers and defended in a philosophical manner. As to what a philosophical manner of defence is, that is a difficult question, though philosophical writing is usually quite easily recognizable as such. One distinguishing mark of philosophical writing, at least as understood in this work, is that on the one hand it proceeds by rather methodical argumentation, and that though it may well appeal to facts of experience, these are facts of experience of a general kind accessible to every reflective human being, and not facts only known through specialized researches. Philosophical thought is largely *a priori*, which means that it purports to be something which one can see to be true simply by thinking about it, without any need for experimentation. As I understand the expression '*a priori*' here, that does not mean that it is thought which dispenses with appeal to experience, but that the experience appealed to is of a universally accessible kind as just indicated. Some may think that philosophical thinking of this sort cannot get us very far, and that to understand the nature of reality we must look to the detailed results of the sciences. Defenders of philosophical theories of existence will claim that scientific research already presupposes a theory of existence adopted on the basis of more general experience. However that may be, there *are* distinctively philosophical theories of existence, and it is the concern of this book to explore some of them. Some of the theories answer only to a limited degree to the account of what a philosophical theory is which I have given, but then they have other features which are recognized as making them philosophical.

In most cases I have discussed the theory of existence as advanced by its main proponent. Most of these theories were originally the view of the world taken by one highly unusual human being, and have a certain personal stamp about them. My concern, however, is with them as points of view upon things which still represent serious options in thinking about the world. Thus though I have liked on the whole to consider them as presented by their first main proponent, where that proponent belongs to the quite distant past, as, for example, in the case of Descartes, I have been concerned with those parts of the theory which are not falsified by virtually indisputable advances in knowledge since his day. I have chosen only theories which, as I see them, are still living options so far as some intelligent people of the present time are concerned. With one exception, each theory is one with which I have some personal sympathy, either as a view I have at some stage been inclined to, or as one which is in some manner incorporated in my own outlook on the world. The exception, which the reader will identify when he comes to it, is there to supply an essential element of balance. In each case my main intention has been to give the most convincing statement of the theory I can. I have regarded myself as a kind of counsel for the defence on its behalf. For this reason I have tried to grasp the essence of the theory in my own mind and then step forward as its momentary advocate, and where I think I can improve upon the original argumentation in its details, while remaining true to its spirit, I have somewhat reformulated matters. Thus the reader must not look in this work for a précis of just what the original author said, but for the most persuasive development of his general line of thought which I can offer. Some criticism of the theories is offered, but this is more because at times I found I could not explain what I thought a theory was getting at except by saying where I thought it was defective, than attack for its own sake.

The thinkers who have been selected as the main representatives of their theory of existence are none earlier in date than the seventeenth century. Since it is obvious from my going back so far that I think there are serious options in the interpretation of existence which have been developed in their main essentials long before the present time, it may be surmised that this is not because I doubt that there are earlier thinkers still whose theories of existence are as worthy of discussion. However, my own particular interest, partly through accident, has not been directed much at thinkers earlier than this time, and, as indicated, I have set out to write a book about theories which have had some particular appeal for me, with the one exception. Actually, the chief thinkers I might have concerned myself with from still earlier times have a merit, which in the present context is a defect: that of being such well-balanced thinkers that one cannot associate them with just one main leading idea, as one can most of the thinkers I have discussed.

The discussion is confined to thinkers in the main tradition of *Western* philosophy. Reasons for this are much those indicated already as the basis of selection.

Each of these theories of existence is one the adoption of which is likely to colour the individual's approach to his or her own personal living of their life. Yet one must not exaggerate the connection between these theories and any particular personal way of life. It is rather that they make the slope up towards some destinations easier than towards others. I have said something about this in each case, though more so in the later chapters. These later chapters are probably a little more humanly vibrant than the earlier ones, but the outlook of the thinkers I consider later cannot possibly be understood without some grasp of the philosophies described in the first three chapters.

This is quite a short book, and the author has had limited time and space and has limited abilities. For this reason I have almost entirely eschewed what is usually called social and political philosophy. So far as the theories of existence discussed point to particular values as those which are of chief importance for human beings, they point to the desirability of forms of social organization in which those values flourish. As to which these are, those who agree on the values may still disagree. It has seemed better to leave distinctively political issues aside, as any treatment of them with the space and ability available to the author would be so superficial as to render it pointless.

The work is intended for those with an interest, actual or arousable, in the kind of philosophic thought which attempts to illuminate what we essentially are, and the real nature of the reality in the midst of which we have our being, but not especially for those with any knowledge of, or training in, philosophy. The order in which I have taken the theories is dictated by the need I have found in explaining one to appeal to another, or by the way in which I see one as capable of resolving problems raised in another, and is not, in all cases, chronological. In particular I see the potentialities of Spinoza's theory of existence for development into a kind of synthesis of most of the other theories as making it suitable for discussion in a final chapter, in spite of the fact that Spinoza himself is one of the earlier thinkers considered.

I have not given page references and so forth to the original works of the theorists of existence, or to commentaries upon these works, in the course of my discussions. These are appropriate in a work of scholarly disputation but would encumber the free flow of the discussion in a way which is unnecessary in a work of the present kind. The reader is warned that others have seen some of these theories of existence in different lights from those in which they are exhibited here. A list of relevant readings in connection with each chapter is given on page 177. These are confined to commentaries, texts and translations in English. Perhaps I should note here that the book deals with two French thinkers, Descartes and Sartre, three German thinkers, Schopenhauer, Nietzsche and Heidegger, and one Dutch thinker, Spinoza, while idealism is mainly represented by the English thinker Bradley, and materialism by the Australian thinker Armstrong.

Acknowledgements

There are various friends and acquaintances in discussion with whom I have enlarged my sense for the significance of the thinkers discussed in this book, but the only quite specific acknowledgement I have to make is to Mr John Llewelyn, who read through the chapter on Sartre and made comments on the basis of which I was able to make my account more accurate on a certain number of points. I also let him see the chapter on Heidegger at rather a late stage and was comforted by his not thinking it quite off the rails, though in neither case do I wish to imply his agreement with my account. I would also like to thank Ted Honderich for his encouragement to write this book and for our many friendly sparrings on philosophic matters.

[ONE]

DESCARTES
AND THEISTIC DUALISM

The first theory of existence which I shall consider is that which received its classic statement in the philosophy of Descartes (1596–1650). In accordance with the general plan of this book, our concern will be with a certain central aspect of this philosophy which is still a living option today. Thus I shall tacitly separate what, as I see it, is still living in Cartesian philosophy from what has an interest rather pertaining only to the history of ideas, and I shall be mainly concerned to put forward the best case for this philosophy I can, criticizing more in the interests of clarification than anything else. In this particular work I shall leave it to the reader to decide for him or herself which theories of existence seem the more satisfactory, though I shall not entirely hide my own sympathies.

The most distinctive element in the Cartesian philosophy ('Cartesianism' being the name of the philosophy of Descartes or Des Cartes) is its contention that a human person is composed of two distinct substances, capable at least in principle of independent existence, the mind and the body. Not only is this thesis, and its implications regarding the relation in which each of us stands to reality in general, of great interest on its own account, but it is also one in relation to which almost every subsequent theorist of existence, including especially those we shall be considering in subsequent chapters, situates his own viewpoint, either positively or negatively.

The view that the human person is made up of two substances, a mind and a body, goes with the more general claim that every single thing which exists is either a mental thing, that is, a mind, or a bodily thing. Cartesianism is, therefore, a dualist theory, according to which a radical and exhaustive division of all that there is can be made into these two categories.

Cartesianism is a theistic philosophy. It holds that everything that there is was created by a single infinite mind, known as 'God', who is also responsible for sustaining everything in existence from moment to moment. As just indicated, God himself is a mind so that he comes under the division of everything into the mental and the physical. However, as its creator he is not part of the created world, and he contrasts with everything in it by his absolute perfection and a certain necessity with which he exists, so that, if one is concerned with the whole of reality, not just the created world, one could represent Cartesianism as dividing realities into three rather than two sorts: two sorts of 'imperfect' things, finite minds and physical things, and things of a 'perfect' sort of which God is the only example. Although God plays an absolutely crucial role in the Cartesian theory, there have been and are atheists who are Cartesians in the sense that they accept a dualism more or less the same as that of Descartes and for more or less the same reasons. In evaluating Cartesian dualism, one should not think of it as necessarily standing or falling with theism.

In my opinion Cartesianism provides a particularly persuasive metaphysical underpinning for Christianity. Descartes himself hoped that his point of view would become the official philosophy of the Roman Catholic Church, to which he belonged. His hope proved vain, for the official philosophy of Roman Catholicism has remained what it was then, Thomism, that is, the philosophical system of St Thomas Aquinas. Yet I believe that many Christians do conceive the world in terms which are largely Cartesian. To me, at least, it seems that Cartesianism offers the best case for saying that man is not essentially a physical organism, and is likely, therefore, to have a destiny beyond this world. So I shall be treating Cartesianism as in some ways supplying the best arguments which a Christian may still use to defend his outlook against typical modern forms of materialism on the one hand, and more Eastern styles of thought on the other.

I should note in passing that Descartes's own main concerns were probably not religious. He was more concerned with developing a new approach to what we would now call scientific inquiry. It remains true that the parts of Cartesianism which are of most interest today, and particularly in connection with the themes of this present book, are those which provide a persuasive alternative to materialism on the one hand, and idealist and mystical theories for which physical reality is an illusion on the other.

Let us now explore the main thesis of Cartesian dualism. My original bald statement of it requires a certain qualification, before we get seriously started. It is not quite the view that everything which exists is either a mind or a physical object, but that every existing substance is. Besides substances there are modes of substance.

This terminology, rooted in medieval thought, and not entirely without currency among philosophers even today, is a little forbidding, but the meaning is fairly straightforward. By a substance is meant a thing in a sense in which the activities and qualities of a thing, and the states it is sometimes in, are not things, while by a mode is meant precisely one of these qualities, activities or states of a thing or substance. These modes are said to exist 'in' the substances to which they pertain, though this metaphorical use of 'in' can be a little puzzling and is at odds with common usage. Thus if I get angry, then my anger is a mode of me said to be *in* me, though ordinary language would lead us to say that it is the person who is *in* the state of anger.

Because it is sometimes convenient, I shall occasionally avail myself of the expressions 'substance' and 'mode'. So let me try to make the meaning clear by inviting the reader who is still puzzled to look out of his window. Perhaps you will see a car or a tree there. These are things or substances. But the car, for example, has a colour or variously distributed colours, it has a shape, and, if it is moving, it has a speed, while if it is not it is in a state of rest. Its colour, shape and speed are modes which are said to be *in* it. They are modes of a physical substance, but they are not substances themselves. The Cartesian holds that minds also, as substances, need to be distinguished from the modes which are in them, such as thinking about something, a desire, or a state of fear, these not being minds, but modes existing *in* a mind. Thus, for Cartesianism, minds and physical objects are the only substances, and everything else which there is must be a mode existing either in a mind or a physical object.

By a body or physical object the Cartesian means essentially something which at any time fills out a position in space. Actually Descartes did not really distinguish between space and the things which are in it. A physical reality is for him something spread out in three dimensions, and since this is true of any part of what we call space, even the apparently most empty space is really a something spread out in three dimensions. But, as indicated in the preface, I am concerned to give an account of each of the theories of existence which I consider in terms which present it as a living option, and for that reason I shall avoid getting bogged down in a precise discussion of just how Descartes conceived the physical. For our purposes we can take it that by a physical thing or substance is meant something filling out a position in space, and take it that in one way or another space pertains to the physical side of things, perhaps as a system of relations in which physical realities stand to each other (relations being some kind of mode), or perhaps as a kind of quasi-physical thing itself. It should be obvious that a particular volume of a liquid or a gas is a physical substance just as much as is a table, tree or machine. There is, indeed, some arbitrariness in the precise way in which we regard total physical reality as dividing up into distinct things. Just because of that the Cartesian has some inclination to think that there is really just one physical substance, the physical universe as a whole, of which all individual things are parts distinguished for some particular purpose.

If there is an element of choice in how we divide the physical up, in our thoughts, into distinct things, this is certainly not true of the mental. Each mind is sharply distinct from every other, at least for the Cartesian. The minds with which we have the most obvious familiarity are human minds, and it is the Cartesian view that though you and I are, from one point of view, each a combination of a mind and a body, still our minds are what we most essentially are, so that when I say 'I' it is a mind which is thus referring to itself. Strictly speaking, when I move about the room it is not the essential I which is moving about, but its body. I have a body, but I am, rather than have, a mind. My mind is not in space in a literal sense, but only in the sense that it has a body which feeds it with information about that body's environment and about itself, and which can be moved about, within limits, by the mind's willing. What the mind, which is what I really am, immediately does is will, perceive, think, feel, and so forth, while physical action is done by the body at the behest, so far as it is voluntary, of the mind.

It is tempting to say that for the Cartesian the mind is related to its body (and it is important to be quite clear that this includes the brain, which is as much something purely physical as is the heart) as a driver is related to his car, while driving. Yet the comparison can be a little misleading, a point which Descartes himself made, talking, of course, not about a driver and his car, but using the example of a pilot and his ship. Not that Descartes's own account of why the analogy is wrong is very satisfactory, since it represents an attempt, perhaps dictated by a wish not to come into too great conflict with the orthodox philosophy of the church, and not too well worked out, to do justice to that intimacy of the relation between mind and body in this life which somehow exists in spite of their distinctness. However that may be, the main reason why the analogy is misleading is that the driver, *qua* physical organism at least, is literally in the car, while the mind is not located somewhere inside the body.

When philosophers of our time discuss Cartesianism, whether they approve of it or not they tend to divide as to how far its view of a human being as made up of distinct realities called mind and body corresponds to 'the common-sense view' of the matter.

One might think that this is of little consequence, and that what matters is whether the Cartesian theory is true. But I think we tend to feel the question important, because we feel the need to have some straightforward view in the background to fall back upon if the philosophers fail us, and which it is their job to persuade us out of if they think it wrong. Yet it is certainly difficult to say what the common-sense view of mind and body is today, in a society such as ours, and whether it is dualistic.

One may surmise that when most people held a religious viewpoint according to which we survive our bodily death, their common sense included a somewhat dualistic conception of their being, for dualism is the doctrine in the light of which life after death seems most likely – though it is not the only conception of mind and body which allows for immortality. Today, however, one can hardly say that common sense necessarily includes such a religious belief, even if it does not exclude it either. Apart from the decline in religious belief, there are various factors which have encouraged materialistic non-dualistic ways of conceiving man. Many people have a more or less vague sense that developments in the understanding of the brain indicate that every detail of mental activity is determined by its structure and states, and are inclined therefore to think that there is no real distinction between the brain and the mind or soul, if the latter term is to continue in use at all. On the other hand, most people surely feel that something is left out, that there is some failure to catch what each of us essentially is, when the attempt is made to capture everything about us in physical terms.

The attempt to chart the relation between Cartesianism and something called common sense is complicated by the fact that the Cartesian use of the actual word 'mind' continues to be unusual. The expressions 'mind' and 'soul' are not synonyms for most people, as they are for the Cartesian, and most people find both expressions a little odd as ways of referring to what they feel themselves essentially to be. One must realize, however, that anyone who thinks that what he most essentially is stands in contrast to his body, and could exist apart from it, as something which has thoughts, feelings, intentions and so forth, is of the Cartesian persuasion whether he calls his essential self a mind, a soul, or whatever. Perhaps we may say that to the extent that there is such a thing as modern 'common sense' it certainly contains a Cartesian element, but that most people are not too happy when the full implications of Cartesianism are spelt out clearly. If I am a Cartesian I must say that strictly speaking I am not in this room and do not have any weight, since these physical concepts are inapplicable to the mind which I am, and this seems rather odd to many people.

From a Cartesian point of view, indeed, there is something almost incurably materialistic about ordinary modes of thought. Thus we all have a tendency if we are told that the mind is without weight and invisible to think of it as a kind of gaseous ghost, held down with difficulty by immurement in the body. For the Cartesian, however, the mind is definitely not a kind of ghostly intruder in the physical world, made of extraordinarily thin stuff. Rather is it something whose whole essence lies in its acts of thought, perception and emotional feeling, and physical conceptions are simply irrelevant to it. The feel of the word 'substance' for most of us militates against realizing this, but one must try to get over that.

Descartes sought to establish the truth of his radically dualistic conception of existence by a line of argument which is as closely knit as any in philosophy. The crux of it lies in the contention that it is conceivable both that the mind should exist without the body, and that the body should exist without the mind, and that this shows that they are distinct things. Furthermore, in conceiving the situation in which my mind exists but my body does not I am conceiving a situation which evidently I should be there to have views about, whereas in conceiving a situation in which my body exists but my mind does not I am conceiving a situation in which there is no question of my being there to have a view about anything, from which it follows that the mind is that one of the two distinct things which is what I essentially am. I can think of myself as a combination of mind and body as long as they are both linked, but the one which can drop out of the picture without myself dropping out of the picture evidently does not belong essentially to that which I am. Let us look at this argument in more detail. Let me make it clear once and for all, both as regards my exposition of Cartesianism and subsequent theories of existence, that I do not set out precisely to duplicate the windings of the author's own published argumentation, but to put what I think to be the essential points in that way I personally find most satisfactory.

In contending that the mind could exist without the body, and vice versa, the Cartesian does not necessarily claim that they do ever exist thus unconnected (though it is beyond doubt that my body will eventually do so as a corpse) but only that it is conceivable that they should do so, that is, that there is nothing radically incoherent in the conception of their doing so. It is not even denied that the system of things, in its actual nature, may totally rule this out as any kind of real or factual possibility. What is in question is logical possibility, which is in fact the same as coherent conceivability, the kind of possibility which pertains, say, to the physical transformation of a Dr Jekyll into a Mr Hyde, as told in the story, even if there is no actual chemical process which would lead to this upshot if tried out. It may seem a rather thin thing to establish that something is logically possible, and yet if in referring to the mind we simply were referring to a part of the body, such as the brain, it would seem to be logically impossible that the mind should exist without this physical thing or structure existing, so that if, contrariwise, this is logically possible it seems that we must be referring to distinct things when we talk, on the one hand, of a mind and on the other of anything physically extended. On the face of it, at least, this is a strong argument. It seems obvious nonsense to point to a tree, a table, or a house and suggest that they may survive their physical destruction and go on existing as themselves, without any question of their somehow being put together again. If it is not similar nonsense to wonder whether the essential you or I may not still exist after our physical destruction, that does look a rather good reason for saying that you and I are not our bodies but that thing, our mind, as the Cartesians will say, which one thereby thinks of as still existing, whether newly embodied or not embodied at all. The force of this argument does not turn on any particular answer to the question whether one is, as mind, so dependent upon one's body, in particular one's living brain, that one cannot survive its destruction. Descartes himself did, of course, believe in life after death and one will only be a partial Cartesian if one does not, but the essential argument for dualism may be accepted by one who denies an actual, as opposed to a conceivable, separability of mind from body, including brain.

It needs to be shown, then, that each of body and mind could exist in separation from the other. As I have said, the existence of corpses shows that the body *does*, and therefore *can*, exist without being connected to its one-time mind. But this is rather less than needs to be shown. For there are many who hold that a human person together with his mind is a living human organism possessed of certain capacities, rather as a working watch is certain constituents put together in such a way and presently adjusted so as to move in a certain manner. We do not say that the watch is something more than a physical thing because it can be destroyed so that it no longer works, and can be so broken up that its constituents no longer make up a watch at all. May it not be, then, that a human person is a certain physical structure behaving in certain ways as a result of what it physically is and the circumstances it is in, and that its mind is simply certain patterns of behaviour it exhibits (thus a kind of physical 'mode')?

In claiming to refute this proposal the Cartesian usually turns to the conceivability of a disembodied mind, but he may also, in line with his general approach, argue the matter from the side of the body. He may contend that absolutely whatever may go on physically inside an organism, or whatever it may physically do, it is logically conceivable that there is no mind pertaining to it. If we are careful in limiting ourselves to the purely physical facts of the case, I may look at another person and think of him as a kind of zombie making certain noises, moving about in certain ways, and with a brain in which complicated physical processes go on in response to stimuli from the environment and which in turn determine his physical behaviour. To think of a human being thus is to think of him as without consciousness, and for the Cartesian, at least, mind and consciousness are one. Even if some of his activities seem to have no adequate physical cause (something unjudgeable indeed by the ordinary observer), I can think of God as making him move about like that as a kind of unconscious puppet. Thus a fully living and normally behaving human organism could conceivably exist without a mind, and in thinking of my friend as having a mind I am therefore supposing something to be there which lies beyond anything which can be captured in a purely physical account.

Descartes himself laid more stress on the conceivability of the mind existing without the body. Part of his case for this lies in suggesting to one the conceivability that one is presently dreaming, and not physically behaving as, or in physical conditions such as, one seems to be. This is the truth about one whenever one is dreaming, and it is not clear but that the whole of one's conscious life might not be a kind of long-term dream. Now just as, looked at from an ordinary point of view, a being of the shape of a man may surely dream that he has the body of a butterfly, while having a rational consciousness, might not a rational being of some quite different shape dream that he had the body of a man, and lived in a society of humans, while his actual body was of some quite different shape? But is it not conceivable that that is just what I actually am, some kind of 'extra-terrestrial' dreaming I have a human body and live in a human civilization, though perhaps there are really no such things in actual existence as human organisms? However far-fetched this may be, unless it is logically impossible it shows that a mind like mine could exist, and have just the experiences it does do, without possessing that body which it seems to itself to possess. But surely we can go further. Surely having once seen that I could, conceivably, have the experiences I do have without possessing this body, I can see that it is conceivable that I am having these experiences without having any body. The fact that I live through a certain series of experiences is one fact. The fact, if it is a fact, that my having these experiences, and perhaps even the existence of this mind or I which has them, is the result of my being in some kind of causal interaction with a body interacting with a certain physical environment, of both of which the images in my consciousness give me a certain picture, is another fact. The second fact offers the most natural interpretation of the first fact, but the holding of the first fact in the absence of the second is a distinct possibility, and shows that I might exist as a mind, having experiences just such as I do have, without possessing a body, and that therefore my mind is something quite other than my body, or any part of it, even granted we cast aside all doubts about the latter's existence.

The conceivability of a mind existing in this way in bodiless fashion is not, perhaps, what people normally try to think of when they think of a purely mental or spiritual existence, for it is an existence in which it is as though I have a body. The Cartesian of any usual sort will, indeed, contend that an existence which not only is, but seems, bodiless is also conceivable.

There are two forms of such explicitly disembodied, or unembodied if there was no previous embodiment, existence which might be in question here. In the first form, there is some kind of sensory experience. It does seem to me conceivable that one should have an experience in which one has visual and other modalities of sense experience which reveal this or some other physical world from shifting points of view which one finds one can alter at will, but without finding any body, observable by oneself or others, which can be called one's own body and which determines one's point of view on things. The oddest aspect of this conception is that all internal bodily feeling presumably has to be thought away, but that does not seem altogether impossible. Perhaps some kind of sense of the filling of the place from which one viewed things might substitute for it, without this being one's body.

Some of what I have just indicated answers to certain reported out-of-the-body experiences. It would remain a very physically orientated sort of existence. A further step towards the conceivability of a mental existence quite removed from the physical sphere lies in what is arguably the quite coherent conception of a mind enjoying the existence of sequences of gorgeous music and nothing else except certain emotional responses thereto, without there being anything which linked that mind, at least during this period, to any physical organism or any part of any physical world.

In claiming that an evidently bodiless existence of either of these sorts is conceivable, I believe that the Cartesian has a strong case. I am sceptical of a further claim which Descartes himself certainly thought important, namely that existence as a mind which thinks about abstract matters, such as logic and algebra, and perhaps even of physical reality through a type of thought which is somehow totally non-sensuous, is conceivable. Even the most abstract thought needs some kind of sensory imagery, visual, auditory, or perhaps of some sensory modality we do not know, as a vehicle of its thinking, and, in fact, I think a being without sensory experience would have nothing to think about. But to talk of experience as sensory is to talk, or so a Cartesian would claim at least, about a certain quality of mental life, and not necessarily to refer to the experience as having a physical source.

If these points are well taken then mind without body is possible, and body without mind. The Cartesian is satisfied that this shows they are distinct types of thing. If it even makes sense to think of X existing without Y, and Y existing without X, it seems to follow that X and Y are not the same thing.

There is, however, an objection to this line of argument. Resting upon this objection, many recent thinkers have claimed that the Cartesian has not shown that the mind may not, after all, really be the very same thing as the brain. Descartes himself was well aware of the possibility of this line of objection, and a more complete account of his argumentation for dualism will show how he thought that he had avoided it.

The objection is that, after all, the fact is that the existence of X without Y may be conceivable, and vice versa, and yet X and Y be the very same thing. For the fact that X and Y are the same thing does not show that it is inconceivable that they should have been different things. The point may be made by a rather simplistic example. One and the same person might be the manager of a certain bank and the leader of a criminal society whom the police are trying to get hold of. It is surely quite conceivable that the manager of the bank and the leader of the society should have been different persons, or that there should have been such a manager without such a criminal leader or vice versa, thus that either one should have existed without the other one doing so. If so, the fact that X might have existed without Y, and vice versa, seems not to show that they are not, in fact, the same entity.

To this the rather complicated Cartesian reply may be suggested briefly as follows. When we identify a thing by a certain linguistic description we normally make it clear what broad sort of thing it is. That means that we indicate something as to the sort of thing it really is in itself, and not just how it is related to something else, and that everything about it as it is in itself can be thought of as its particular way of being a thing of that sort. Thus if I speak of something as being a prime number which lies between six and ten, meaning thereby to refer to the number seven, I have indicated that it belongs to the broad category of numbers, a category of the right sort inasmuch as everything true about the number seven may be regarded as its particular way of being a number. Such a way of referring to the number seven contrasts with a reference to it as the entity used as an example on page 23 of this book, which does not indicate the broad sort of thing it is in itself, but identifies it in a much more extrinsical way. Now what the Cartesian says is that a thing X and a thing Y cannot be the same thing if each of them could conceivably exist out of any sort of real relation to anything of that broad sort of thing of which the other is an example.

This will be clearer when we look to our actual examples. It looks as though when I refer to my body in a manner which makes it clear what sort of thing it is I indicate that it is something which exists by filling out space, while when I similarly refer to my mind I indicate that it is something which exists by thinking and having experiences, and so forth. The Cartesian claims to have shown, in the manner we have outlined, that it is conceivable that my mind should exist out of all real relation to anything which fills out space, while my body could likewise exist (and even exist as an ordinarily behaving human organism) without any real relation to anything which thinks and has experiences. If that is right, then each is capable of existing independently of anything of the broad sort of thing of which the other is an example. Obviously this is not so in the case of the bank manager and the criminal, since presumably the broad sort of thing of which each is an example is a human being, and a human being is at the least in a real relation to himself.

The discussions to which philosophers have been led in trying to evaluate this line of thought have often been very complex, and we cannot explore the matter much further. In my opinion the Cartesian case is made out if it is true that my mind could exist without any real relation to a body, including a brain, and vice versa, and the crucial question is whether this has actually been made out.

One reason why many have been reluctant to accept that it has been made out lies in the sceptical conclusions about human knowledge which seem to follow in that case. It is well known that it was a particular interest of Descartes both to exhibit the force of scepticism and to offer a reply to it, but he is usually thought of as more successful in doing the former than the latter.

The difficulty is, of course, that if it really is conceivable that I should have just the experiences I do have and not have a body or be in any connection with a real physical world, it is not at all clear what justification I have for my normal confidence about these matters. Or, to take up an aspect of the matter which Descartes himself hardly considers, supposing I grant that I am embodied and perceiving and acting via my body in a real physical world, how can I be sure that the other human organisms around me are not zombies without minds, if it is, as contended, conceivable that they might be? The feeling that if dualism is true, then the fact that I belonged to a community of embodied minds, inhabiting by way of their bodies a real physical world, could never be something I really knew of but at best would be a mere guess, has led many philosophers to look for a conception of mind and body according to which their being is not even conceivably separable. We shall be touching on some of these conceptions in later chapters. Here we must briefly note the Cartesian response to scepticism.

Descartes's own reply can be summed up briefly. First he develops the famous 'Cogito ergo sum' ('I think therefore I am') theme. There are various alternative ways in which what he says in this connection has been understood. I shall take it as simply the invitation to every conscious being to note that in every act of thinking, feeling or willing it performs it is conscious of itself as doing so, and thus conscious of itself as existing. This means that each mind knows with absolute certainty what it is thinking, what ideas it has, whatever doubts it may have as to whether anything real exists beyond its own mental contents which corresponds to these ideas. His next step is to claim that each of us can know that he has or can form the idea of a perfect being we may call God, and he then claims that the idea of God is distinguished from all other ideas in that merely by reflecting on it we see that there must be a reality outside our minds corresponding to it. God's existence having been proved, allegedly,

Descartes claims that God, as a good being, would not have given us experiences which prompt us to beliefs which we cannot replace by any better grounded ones, unless these beliefs were true.

I shall consider shortly the reason the Cartesian gives for claiming that God's existence can be inferred from one's idea of Him. But first I want to insist that many thinkers today are dualists who entirely reject the Cartesian reasons for believing in God, and have therefore to look for another answer to scepticism. (They may or may not believe in God, but they would not argue for his existence in this way and for this purpose.) What they would usually say about scepticism is that worry about it arises from a quest for a kind of absolute certainty which is unrealistic. We should be content to accept that interpretation of our experiences which seems to make the best sense of them, even if its truth is not absolutely guaranteed but only in some sense probable, and that means that we should interpret the experiences which suggest to us that we are embodied and in contact within a physical world with other embodied beings as being in fact caused in this way. The fact that this is not certain shows us the distinctness of mind and body but need not plunge us into serious scepticism.

Although people are often interested in Cartesian philosophy for the sceptical problems it raises, that is not our main concern with it. We are concerned rather with the positive account of reality which it offers, as consisting of just two sorts of thing or substance, minds and physical objects, and of an infinite mind, God, which created and continuously sustains everything else in being. For that reason I turn now to the Cartesian argument for God's existence, not in order to evaluate the cogency of appealing to God's existence as a way of answering scepticism about the existence of the physical world and so forth, but simply for its interest as a way of trying to establish that there really is a God.

There are two main Cartesian attempts to prove the existence of God. The first invites us to acknowledge that, whether we believe in God's existence or not, we can at least form the idea of such a being. More specifically, I can form the idea of a mind which lacks all the limitations to which I, as a mind, am subject, one which knows everything, has everything within its power, and is totally good. Descartes even insists that I only realize that I am limited, for example in my knowledge, because I can contrast myself with a being which would be unlimited, so that awareness of my own limitations carries with it the ability to form the idea of God. He then goes on to contend, in a manner I shall not follow in detail, that the idea of God is such an infinitely magnificent idea that it could only have come into the human mind through the operation of a really existing God. Even if one got the idea of God from one's parents, there must be an explanation of how it first originated in a human mind at all, and, in fact, my parents could only elicit the idea in me if it was implicitly there already, and this requires that it have been put there by an actual God.

People today are inclined to respond to this argument by referring to explanations of the origin of the idea of God offered by certain psychologists and sociologists. Freud held that the idea of God was the idea of a glorified father figure, in which the feelings we have towards our father are internalized, while sociologists have sometimes suggested that the idea of God is an internalized feeling of the demands of our tribe or society. Probably the Cartesian argument, just as it stands, will seem unconvincing to most. One might modify it to the claim that the best explanation for the origin of this idea in human minds does lie in the existence of an actual God, a claim which would need to be supported by establishing at length the inadequacy of other explanations. In doing so, we should be modifying Cartesianism towards a claim about what is probable in the way already indicated when we discussed how modern Cartesians, dissatisfied with the role Descartes calls upon God to play in dealing with them, would usually face the apparently sceptical implications of dualism.

The second Cartesian argument is really more interesting. It is known as the ontological argument, and had been put forward previously, in a somewhat different form, by the twelfth-century archbishop of Canterbury, St Anselm.

In coming to grips with this argument it is helpful to start by asking what is going on when we ask whether something exists or not. This can seem a problem, for presumably we must know what it is concerning the existence of which we are asking, and must somehow be referring to it. But if it is a something to which we can refer, must it not in some sense *be*? Yet surely it is the question whether there is such a thing with which we are concerned.

In response to this, many philosophers, Cartesians among them, say that we are referring to a certain essence, as they call it, and asking whether it is actualized. A thing which exists is an actualized essence, a thing which does not exist is an unactualized essence. When we ask whether a thing exists or not we are referring to an essence in a manner which leaves it open, until the question is answered, whether it is actualized or not. Considered merely as an essence, which may not be actualized, that essence has, indeed, a kind of being, but does not, in the usual sense, exist.

The essence may be a partial or a complete essence. When I ask whether unicorns exist I refer to a partial essence which would be an element in the complete essence of any actual unicorn, did one exist. Even when I ask whether one certain single thing exists, my immediate reference is to a partial essence. The essence I refer to when I ask whether the Loch Ness monster exists could not be the complete essence of that supposedly single being, did it exist. (Perhaps people do not really mean to imply that there is only one, but it will do as an example.)

It would be a mistake to confuse an essence with the idea of the essence which exists in the mind of one who thinks about it. For the non-existence of something may be a fact even if no one knows about that fact, so that, so to speak, there must then be an essence which fails to be actualized, even when there is no idea of that thing in any mind. If we suppose that God knows concerning every possible thing whether it exists or not we may see reasons for identifying essences with ideas in God's mind, but certainly not with ideas in finite minds.

The question whether something exists or not is the question whether a certain essence is actualized or not. In most cases we cannot discover the answer to the question simply by scrutinizing the essence itself as revealed to us in our idea of it. Some kind of observation or inference from observation is necessary for deciding that the essence horse is actualized and the essence unicorn is not. However, there are some essences we only have to think about to see that they are not, because they could not be, actualized. The essence which would be actualized in any round square, were there such things, is a customary example.

Are there any essences such that mere reflection on them in thought shows that they must be actualized, and that therefore they are actualized in really existing things? According to the ontological argument there is one such essence, the essence of the divine being, the essence which if it is actualized, or granted that it is, is God himself. Or, rather, there is just one complete essence such that for one who grasped it conceptually it would be clear that it is necessarily actualized as God himself, while there may be various partial essences, which are elements of this complete essence, and which exhibit themselves to one who grasps them as elements which must be actualized in some complete divine essence.

If we can even ask the question whether God exists we have in our minds some essence which, if actualized, is God himself, or an essential element in his being. The atheist cannot deny that he has the idea of a divine essence. If he did not have such an idea his statement that God does not exist would be of the character of the nonsensical statement 'Bongwong does not exist'. This statement, however, having a word in the subject position without any significance, not even referring to something self-contradictory like a round square, is neither true nor false, while the atheist thinks his denial of God's existence is true.

The proponent of the ontological argument claims to be able to see, by consideration of the essence which one is thinking of when one asks whether God exists or not, that just as the essence of a round square is one incapable of being actualized, so this divine essence is one which is incapable of not being actualized. The nub of his argument is this. An essence which could pertain uniquely to a being worthy to be called God would have to be a perfect essence. Even the atheist should admit that this divine essence, the actualization of which he denies, is perfect, as being that which, if it were actualized, would pertain to a perfect being. But surely an essence which might just as well not be actualized would not in this manner be perfect. Surely it is one of the marks of one's own imperfection and finitude that there is no intrinsic reason why one should not have failed to exist (something not conflicting with the fact that granted I do exist I register this fact in myself with absolute certainty). This is as much as to say that any essence pertaining uniquely to me might very well not have been actualized. In contrast to this, any essence which could pertain uniquely to God must be a perfect essence which could not fail to be actualized. Thus if I think about the matter hard enough I will realize that in grasping the very meaning of the expression 'God' I see that it signifies a perfect essence which must be actualized in the being of an actually existing God.

Reams have been written concerning this argument (presented in a somewhat different fashion by Descartes himself). The person who dismisses it quite summarily as sheer nonsense has probably failed quite to take it in. which is not to deny that when a reasonable understanding of it has been grasped it may be dismissed as ultimately specious. I do not want to step forward here as one whose views about it should especially influence the reader in assessing it, but shall briefly suggest a point of view on it to which a number of wise heads have inclined.

If God does exist, it seems he must necessarily exist. There must be something about his essence or nature which is such that a proper grasp of it would show that it could not have failed to be actualized. The alternative would be to suppose that even if God does exist, there is no explanation for the fact that he exists. For if there is an explanation of

God's existence it must lie in his own nature, since everything else, granted he does exist, issues from, or has been created by, him. But even if he does exist in this way it is perfectly possible that we do not have sufficient grasp of his full essence to see what it is about it which makes it impossible that it should not have been actualized. Our conception of God may be by way of a partial essence which does not exhibit on its own, or to us, this so to speak self-actualizing power which belongs to the complete divine essence in which it belongs as an element. And that, if God does exist, seems to be the actual case, since one surely cannot really see any incoherence in the assertion that God does not exist as one can, say, in the assertion that round circles do.

If that is right we cannot settle whether God exists on the basis of the essence which is present to our thoughts when we think about him. We must decide whether he exists or not on other grounds, or leave the matter open. But we can say that if he does exist then there must, so to speak, be an ontological argument available to *him* (and to any other mind which has an adequate grasp of his essence), since to suppose that he exists is to suppose that he is the actualization of some (to us in its totality unknown) perfect essence which could not have failed to be actualized, in contrast to beings like us, whose essence, even in its completeness, has nothing which makes the idea that it might never have been actualized absurd.

Before rounding off this account of Cartesianism by considering its wider ramifications, I must clarify a niggling point of detail. In speaking of the way in which we normally indicate the broad category of entity to which something of which we speak belongs, I referred to the category of numbers. How do these come in on a scheme for which everything that is belongs either to the category of minds or bodies or is some kind of mode existing in one or other of these?

Some philosophers, whether Cartesians or not, regard numbers, things like five and seven and a half and a quarter, together with other things usually classified along with them as abstract entities, as a kind of fiction. Another view, approximating to Descartes's own, is that they are a kind of mode capable of occurring in both the physical and mental realm as in some sense 'in' groups of minds or physical things. Or perhaps they are some kind of essence, perhaps the essence of certain modes. The question is difficult, and need not much concern us in discussing theories of existence. For these are theories about what exists in some more full-blooded or concrete way than abstract entities like numbers exist, if they do exist in any proper sense. It is worth noting in this connection that the fact that minds, including God himself, exist in *non-physical fashion* does not mean that they are abstract entities like numbers, which surely are in some sense simply aspects of the way in which more properly existing things exist.

It is time to ask what effect adoption of the Cartesian theory of existence is liable to have upon a person's general attitude to life.

I suggested earlier that Cartesianism serves well as a metaphysical underpinning of Christian belief which may confirm a Christian in his faith, or lead a non-Christian towards it. For Cartesianism supposedly establishes the existence of God and of the individual person as non-physical in his essential being. If one is satisfied that this is so, one may think it likely that God has revealed his purposes in some way, and indicated a destiny which may await us after death. Searching for a revelation, one may decide that one of the religions claiming to be revealed is the true one. That might form the basis for becoming a Christian, or perhaps for accepting the claims of another religion purporting to be revealed. I shall not pursue these possibilities, which would take us way beyond the more specifically Cartesian outlook.

Whether one joins a religious faith or not, a Cartesian conception of reality is liable to encourage a particular slant on what is really valuable in existence. For the Cartesian I am most essentially my mind. Mind here means conscious mind since it is mind as consciousness the separability of which from body is supposed to have been exhibited. (We shall see how a modern Cartesian regards the unconscious when we come to Sartre.) That suggests that what really matters for me is the quality of my existence as a mind, and that my body should be regarded as of value only as a support to this.

Regarding the mind as one thing, and the body as another, the Cartesian tends to distinguish even within the activity and states of the mind those which spring from its own inherent nature, and those which reflect rather its relation to a body. We have seen that for the Cartesian it is theoretically possible that any kind of sense experience whatever could exist in a mind without a body; none the less granted we do have bodies the Cartesian sees sense experience as due particularly to the mind's being yoked to a body, while intellectual activity and perhaps certain purely spiritual experiences are due more to the mind's own nature. Identifying himself with the mind as he does, the Cartesian is inclined, therefore, to see these supposedly less bodily conditioned aspects, of his existence as a mind, as those which should concern him most, especially as they are the ones he is likely to be left with if he survives bodily death.

Thus Cartesianism tends to lead to a low evaluation of the pleasures or goods of the body, as we normally put it, and this is usually taken to include not only the pleasures of eye, ear, sex and the table but also emotions which seem to overcome us as a result of our bodily being. Descartes, indeed, tended to identify everything he thought of as disreputable, such as anger, as representing the influence of the body on the mind, and put great stress upon will power in his ethics, since he saw will as above all the assertion of the mind's own nature against what comes to it from the body.

It seems, then, that the way of life which a Cartesian is most likely to espouse is one in which true satisfaction is seen as lying in intellectual activity or spiritual meditation and in which one frees oneself so far as possible from what stems from one's bodily being, something which may even include social preoccupations, since one belongs to society only through one's body. Moreover, the Cartesian, because he sharply distinguishes the true person from his body, will be less inclined to accept that a person lacks freedom to resist bodily temptation. Presumably a modern Cartesian will be less likely to accept the view that genetic determination has made someone, say, a criminal without the option, since seeing the person as essentially a mind he will believe he had the freedom to resist inclinations which came to him from his bodily inheritance.

This kind of attitude to human life was powerfully espoused towards the beginning of Western philosophy by Plato, and received a more extreme formulation some centuries later in the neo-Platonist philosophy of Plotinus. It is because Cartesianism is, in this respect, so Platonist that many Christians reject its claim to be a Christian philosophy, maintaining that Christianity does not in this way identify man's true being with his mind. This, however, depends very much on what aspect of Christianity one emphasizes.

There is no doubt that the kinds of reason I have been considering for insisting on the distinctness of mind and body have been used to support a view of things in which our bodily being is devalued. However, the movement of thought is by no means logically compulsive. One could, after all, hold that the mind is at its best when shot through with influences which come to it from the body. Besides, the tendency to devalue bodily being on the basis of a dualistic theory of the human person is, above all, a tendency to devalue the goods of sensory experience as against some supposedly more purely intellectual or spiritual mode of mental being, and this turns on the weakest part, as it seems to me, of Cartesianism, namely the view that a mind is conceivable which has no kind of sensory experience whatever. As against this, as I suggested earlier, it seems that even if some sort of unembodied existence is conceivable it still has to include something of the nature of sensory experience. If I am right, it cannot be reasonable to think that mind should aspire to some kind of purely spiritual or intellectual good, divorced from sense experience, since sense experience pertains to the essence of mind as truly as the capacity for abstract thought. It may even pertain to it more truly. Granted that animals have minds, we may take it that these are more deeply immersed in sense experience than ours, and have less capacity for abstract thought.

Descartes, actually, denied that animals had minds, and regarded them as unconscious automata. He may have favoured this view as removing ethical objections to vivisection, which he practised in his own research, but it also reflects that tendency to see abstract thinking as the essence of mind, which, I have contended, belongs to the weaker side of his thought.

Indeed, the whole tendency to devalue the goods of physical existence on the basis of a dualistic theory of existence turns on the less well-supported side of Cartesianism. The reasons it gives for saying that mind or consciousness is a distinct reality from anything physical are very strong. They do not, however, show that these genuinely distinct realities may not be so related that the one is totally dependent on the other. They do not rule out, for example, the doctrine of epiphenomenalism, that conscious mind arises only when there is a brain in a certain state and that every state and act of mind is caused by a state of the brain in such manner that the mind really has no independent power of acting. There may be reasons for rejecting this view, but the main Cartesian arguments for dualism we have considered do not suffice.

In contrast to such weaker forms of dualism as epiphenomenalism, Cartesian dualism, in the full sense, is known as interactionism. As such it insists not only that mind or consciousness is something totally distinct from anything physical, but also that mind and body are two powers interacting on a par; mind, indeed, having more power over body, when it is determined to resist its blandishments, than it likes to admit when excusing its succumbment to temptation. In order to decide whether interactionism is true or not, one would need to evaluate an enormous mass of data from such contrasting areas as neuro-physiology and psychical research. If we are persuaded by the crucial Cartesian arguments which we have been exploring that mind and body are certainly utterly distinct kinds of thing, we must look to these and kindred fields of research to decide between interactionist dualism or one of a more epi-phenomenalist character.

Some people who accept these arguments for the distinctness of mind and body contend that the presumption must be very strongly in favour of interactionism rather than epiphenomenalism. They see it as an absurdity that our minds should have (or consist of) experiences which are totally determined by what goes on in our bodies (or more specifically our brains) while what occurs in our minds makes no difference to what our bodies do at all.

Doubtless these people are right in thinking this idea an odd one, but it is doubtful whether it really suffices as a ground for dismissing the epiphenomenalist version of dualism from serious consideration. Certainly it has had some very astute advocates, most notably the American philosopher George Santayana (1863–1952).

[TWO]

MATERIALISM

For dualism every existing thing is either a mind, a physical object, or a mode of one of these, that is a state, act, quality (or whatever) of one of these. The next two theories of existence stand in a simple relation to dualism, since each is arrived at by simply dropping one of these two sorts of thing, either entirely or by treating it as some kind of mode of the other. Materialism, the topic of this chapter, says that all that exists is physical things and their modes; idealism, the topic of the next, says that all that exists is the mental and its modes. We should be clear that a mode of the physical cannot be something essentially non-physical which somehow issues from the physical, but must be a genuinely physical aspect of the physical's being, such as a thing's movement in space, and a similar remark applies to a mode of the mental, when we come to idealism.

In popular parlance, a materialist is someone concerned with so-called material goods or values rather than with so-called spiritual ones. Thus one may be called a materialist because one shows oneself more concerned to acquire material possessions than a virtuous disposition, or one may be called a materialist because one's vision of the good society is one in which there is a high level of physical comfort and undemanding entertainment, rather than one in which there is a high level of cultural and intellectual achievement. A philosophical materialist is not necessarily a materialist in either of these senses, which I have heard a philosophical materialist designate in contrast as 'washing-machine materialism'. We shall consider later whether philosophical materialism does point to an ethic of washing-machine materialism, but for the present it is solely philosophical materialism which concerns us.

One sometimes encounters a mistaken identification of materialism and atheism. However, there is nothing especially problematic about an atheist who is not a materialist. We have seen that atheism is compatible with dualism, for example.

There is, indeed, something a little odd in a combination of theism with materialism, though there have been thinkers of this persuasion. The difficulty is the apparent necessity of thinking of God as a physical being. A complete materialist who believed in God would presumably have to think of God as a physical being. The alternatives seem to be thinking of God as a kind of super physical organism controlling things from outer space or identifying him with the physical world. But to use 'God' to refer to something of the first kind is to take God as a merely glorified animal, and that is not a proper use of the word 'God' as its meaning has developed since the growth of Christianity, while it is equally inept merely to use the word as a name for the totality of the physical world (unless that is thought of as also having non-physical characteristics which make it divine, as in the philosophy of Spinoza, which is not materialist, though it does in a manner think that the physical universe is God). An alternative kind of theistic materialism might say that the created world is totally physical, though God is not. But then it is difficult to see how there could be anything in the created world supplying us with a clue to the existence of this non-physical God. So although it is not a self-contradiction in any straightforward way, I shall take it that in effect to be a materialist is to be an atheist. What is not true is that to be an atheist is necessarily to be a materialist.

There have been five main groups of materialist thinkers in Western thought: (1) the ancient Greek atomists, in particular Democritus and Epicurus; (2) certain seventeenth- and eighteenth-century materialists, such as Hobbes and Gassendi; (3) certain influential philosophers of our own time whom I shall call analytical materialists, because they are working in the tradition of what is called analytical philosophy; (4) the dialectical materialism of Marx, Engels and subsequent Marxists; (5) emergent materialism, which I think has no outstanding spokesmen.

I shall group the first three together under the heading of standard materialism. It is that with which I shall be mainly concerned, and the expression 'materialism' will stand for this when not otherwise indicated.

The ancient Greek atomists thought that the world consisted of an infinite number of minute indestructible atoms or particles of various different shapes, whirling about in space, or falling continually down in it. Ordinary visible and tangible things consisted for them of aggregations of these atoms held together by an interlocking of their shapes. Liquids and gases were looser aggregations of such atoms. The minds or spirits of organisms consisted of some kind of similarly composed fluid or gas circulating through the body and taking on the shapes of things imping-ing on the sense organs, thereby somehow constituting the organism's awareness of its environment. The details of their theories were ingenious, but far removed from anything we now accept as scientific fact. More-over, the method by which they were reached was speculation largely untested by experiment and not scientific in a modern sense. Nor was there the kind of attempt at demonstrative argument by which dualists have sought to establish their case. The same is largely true of Hobbes, Gassendi, etc. Thus, while it remains the best way of approaching dual-ism, and other theories we shall turn to later, to follow close on its first careful formulation, if materialism is to be considered as a living option we must turn to the way in which it is developed by modern thinkers. Yet the ancient atomists, and above all the Roman follower of Epicurus, Lucretius, still give the most inspiring presentation of the essential materialist vision of the world and of the emotions it calls forth.

For the materialist everything is physical or material (expressions which here are synonymous). But what is it about a thing which marks it as physical? Perhaps we will not go far wrong if we stick to the account we gave in the previous chapter and say that a physical thing is some-thing which fills out a position in space and that its physical modes are simply aspects of that filling out of a space which a physical thing essen-tially is, or its movements in space or perhaps some aspect of them. As for space itself, we must regard it either as a kind of extra quasi-physical thing allowed for in the materialistic scheme of things, or as some kind of relation in which physical things stand to each other so that the filling out of space is a matter of how a thing's parts stand to each other or how it as a whole stands to other things. Perhaps there are things which should be called physical not answering quite to this specification, but I think they would answer to some account which is a sophistication rather than an abandonment of this.

The standard materialist not only thinks that everything is physical but also holds that everything which happens, so far as it is explicable at all, is explicable by physical laws which hold pervasively throughout the world, as does the law of gravitation for Newtonian physics. Thus he will think that the growth of plants and the behaviour of animals is ultimately explicable (whether we know the explanation or not) by the same laws that govern what happens throughout the inanimate world, only of course they are governing a different arrangement of the more basic constituents of matter, arrangements whose existence was brought about by the earlier operation of those same laws. This will be true of thought itself, which for the materialist must somehow be a physical process going on, it would be taken for granted now, within the brain.

The dialectical and the emergent materialist deny that everything is governed by physical laws applicable throughout nature. They believe that when the ultimate constituents of matter get into certain sorts of arrangements, as for example in organisms, they start behaving in ways which must be subsumed under irreducibly different laws. That does not necessarily mean that anything is going on other than a new kind of behaviour on the part of the same basic physical constituents, though they seem sometimes to hold that something radically new then turns up to fill out space. If, however, not merely new laws, which is to say, really, new habits of movement or new fillings of space, are invoked, but the influence of something not thus filling out a space at all, we have a departure, inadvertent or otherwise, from anything which it is appropriate to call materialism. There is nothing contrary to materialism, however, in thinking that there is an element of sheer randomness in the world, and that the most fundamental laws holding at certain levels are statistical, so that in certain cases there is no explanation at all of why things happened in one precise way rather than another. This is implied by modern physics and is equally compatible with standard materialism.

In saying that everything is physical, the materialist wishes to deny something which some people believe. But what exactly is it which he is saying does not exist which others think does exist? One cannot say that it is mind. Usually at least, though there are exceptions, the materialist will certainly deny that he is out to deny the existence of our minds. No, what he wants to say is that we do have minds but that really somehow or other our minds are physical realities. The mental is simply a special kind of complication in the physical world. What he is denying is that there is such a thing as an immaterial mind. Still, from the point of view of the dualist, whether the materialist admits as much himself or not, he is denying the existence of the mind in any proper sense.

What about other things to which we might be inclined to attribute a non-physical existence? In most cases the materialist deals with them as he does with the mind. He tries to show, not that there are no such things, but that really they are physical. Examples might be art, tradition, languages, cultures, each of which is sometimes thought of as having an existence of a non-physical kind.

In the previous chapter I referred to numbers, like three and five, as entities which do not seem either to be minds or physical objects, and which might therefore cause a difficulty for dualism. I suggested that in some sense not too easy to explain these are abstract objects, and that the dualist is really concerned only to say that all things which exist in a more full-blooded and concrete way are either minds or physical objects. As for numbers, he might try to treat them as modes of mind or the physical, or he might dismiss them as a kind of fiction, or deal with them in some other way. Much the same applies to materialists. Some see numbers and other purely abstract entities as modes of the physical, some dismiss them as a kind of fiction, while others admit that they are not physical but say that materialism asserts only that all *concrete* realities are physical. Perhaps the most plausible view for the materialist is to say that numbers are somehow either actual or possible modes which do or might exist as an aspect of the physical being of groups of physical things. If they are regarded as things which exist independently of any groups of things to which they apply they really become a kind of essence. But can the materialist admit essences? There is really no reason why not. An essence is effectively a logical possibility which might or might not be actualized. Thus the essence of a tiger is a possible combination of characteristics which may be actualized in some real beast. The materialist need not deny that there are unactualized possibilities like unicorns which have a kind of being without being physically real. To safeguard the essentials of his materialism, all he need insist is that every actual thing is physical, and that either there is simply no genuine possibility whose actuality would be something non-physical, or that if in some sense there are non-physical possibilities there is something about the world which in practice rules out their actualization.

The above paragraph may leave the reader somewhat puzzled, as I have had to pass over a large issue quickly. The main point is that materialism, like other theories of existence, is concerned with what exists not in the thin and abstract way that a number does, but in some much more full-blooded way. Note that something which exists as a mode of something physical is not abstract in the sense that an abstract number, which is not the number of any particular group of things, is. The shape of a particular single object is abstract in one sense in contrast to the thing as a whole, but is not an abstraction in the sense in which I have used the term.

Clearly the main problem for materialism is as to the nature of the mind. There are some materialists today who take the extremely tough line that really there is no such thing as the mind or even mental activities or states. The whole thing simply belongs to a mythical stage of human thought and will eventually die out as anything to be taken seriously. Mind will belong with the gorgons and harpies. This point of view is sometimes called eliminative materialism. But even its spokesmen are bound to find it difficult to grasp how people will speak when their thought is thoroughly demythologized – will it even be proper on their part to speak of their thought?

Most materialists take a somewhat more sober approach. Certainly, they say, human beings, and doubtless animals, have minds. Indeed, we may be more generous still, many of them hold, and say that an adequately programmed computer has a mind, and mechanisms which man will learn to produce will have minds in a fuller way still. None the less, these minds are nothing immaterial. The word 'mind' belongs to a somewhat different level of discourse from the language in which we all recognize ourselves as talking about the physical; none the less in talking of mind what we are actually referring to is physical.

Let us see how the materialist vindicates his position in this connection. The most plausible approach is that of contemporary analytical materialists, and it is their account that I shall follow. Not that they are in entire agreement with one another, but I shall distil a line of thought which should give an adequate idea of the general point of view. I shall be drawing especially on the writings of David Armstrong, author of *A Materialist Theory of the Mind* (1968), though my account will also contain elements drawn from other writers.

The materialist of this kind emphasizes the need to distinguish the question whether the concepts expressed by different linguistic expressions are equivalent, from the question whether the entities they apply to are different things. A pound note is a piece of paper exhaustively describable at one level in terms of its physical make-up. It is as physical a thing as anything could be. On the other hand, a description of it in terms of the paper it is made of, the shapes which are somehow imprinted on it, ultimately the molecules which make it up, does not exhibit that feature about it which makes it a pound note. So the expression 'a pound note' does not exactly tell us what this piece of paper's physical nature is, but the thing which answers to that expression is a physical entity. 'This piece of paper' and 'this pound note' are expressions with a different kind of meaning, that is, they express quite sharply contrasting concepts, which refer to the same individual physical thing.

On this point dualists, materialists and many others would, mostly agree. The dualist, however, would probably say that though a pound note is itself a physical thing, what makes it a pound note is a fact about how certain human minds have come to an agreement about the rights bestowed upon one who has hold of it, other than through violence, or rather bestowed upon one who has hold of any physical thing of this sort with a certain origin. Thus it is a pound note in virtue more of its relations to mind than in virtue of its physical make-up. The materialist may agree with this, but in order to support his materialism he must somehow show that these minds and the relations in which they stand to pound notes are physical. How this is done we are going to see, but the initial point to be made does not turn on a resolution of this problem, but only on acknowledging that the very same thing may fall under radically different sorts of concept, as exhibited in the case of the pound note. One other moral he would have us draw from the simple example of the pound note is that though pound notes do have certain rather definite physical characteristics, things with pretty different characteristics might have functioned in the same way, and been pound notes instead of pieces of paper of this sort. For example, the pound note could be, and at the time of writing actually is going to be, replaced by a coin. Probably it will not then be referred to as a note, but one can imagine that the same expression 'pound piece' might have been used of the note and transferred without change to the coin.

In the light of this the materialist points out that all that is really acceptable in the Cartesian argumentation can be incorporated in a materialist scheme for which the brain and the mind are regarded as the same physical thing, though the expression 'brain' points to its physical characteristics, while the expression 'mind' points to certain relations in which it stands to other things.

The Cartesian holds that body could exist without anything mental existing whatever. But could one not say that pound pieces might exist without any paper existing, if pound pieces had been coins from the start? Does that show that pound pieces are not, as a matter of fact, made of paper? Similarly, the materialist will say, things physically composed (perhaps even with the same internal processes going on within them, though here most materialists will hesitate) just as brains are, human brains in particular, might exist at some time when there are no minds, but that does not show that brains in the appropriate relations with other things are not minds. Thus the general lines of a reply to this side of the Cartesian argument are laid out.

The Cartesian also holds that minds could exist without anything physical existing. Well, is this not just the straight converse of the other case? Obviously pieces of paper of the exact physical nature of a pound note could exist without pound pieces existing, for example in a society without money but which used such pieces of paper as a decoration. Still, it is a little more difficult for the materialist to carry the analogy over to the actual case of his concern. To do so he will say first that, after all, that which is related to other things so as to be a mind might not have been physically that like a brain. It might have been made of metal and wire or silicon chips, like a computer. That, however, does not show how minds could have existed without anything physical at all. So the materialist says that although in his opinion there is nothing which is not physical, still there might have been, and that things made up of whatever this non-physical reality would have been, might have been related to other things, likewise composed of something non-physical, and then there would have been mind existing in detachment from everything physical. Alternatively, he might say that though the Cartesian is right that a mind might conceivably have existed as a mind without itself having any physical existence, it would have been bound to have some kind of relation to physical things, and would have been a mind because these were of the right sort.

To this the dualist will object that what makes something a mind is not the manner in which it is related to things not somehow implicit in its own being, but something much more intrinsic. But the materialist challenges this by suggesting a certain account of what, on reflection, we are supposed to realize is really meant by the expression 'mind' together with all expressions for mental processes, states and so forth, such as 'perception', 'desire', 'emotion' and such like.

According to the materialist, what we mean when we talk of a human organism's mind is something which plays a distinctive role in causing that organism's behaviour, in a manner which is continually subject to modification, in a way which usually assists the organism's survival, or 'welfare', by the stimuli reaching its sense organs from the environment. All the expressions for particular mental states indicate that that something called the mind is in some state calculated to influence behaviour in some particular direction, or that its influence on behaviour is being modified by the influence on it of particular stimuli from the environment which have reached it either just now or in the more distant past. Thus to say that the mind contains a desire to eat cherries is to say that it is in some state which is liable to produce the placing of cherries in the mouth followed by consumption, in a manner subject to suitable influence by present and past stimulation of its sense organs. To say that it contains a certain memory is to refer to a state which modifies present behaviour as a result of certain past stimuli and so forth. The detailed treatment of particular mental states, as elaborated particularly by David Armstrong in the book mentioned above, along these general lines has been extremely ingenious, but cannot be followed up here. We may just note, however, that desire and will are key aspects of the mind and that there is of course nothing so crude as a simple identification of a desire with something which tends to produce certain results, else one would have to say that when clouds burst they desire to help the crops. No, a desire is a state which produces behaviour with a certain tendency to produce a certain result, where the precise behaviour is continually modified in the manner most likely to produce that result granted the organism's sense organs are being affected as they are. But though the clouds do not have a desire to assist the crops, the behaviour of a homing rocket or Exocet missile is caused by something which is at least a crude kind of desire, for it is so constructed that the stimuli which reach it from the environment, and thereby affect the internal but purely physical mapping of the location of objects around it which it contains, do modify its direction so as to make a certain definite upshot more likely, if not deadly certain.

So one's mind is simply whatever it is inside or otherwise pertaining to one which initiates one's more complex goal-directed behaviour under the influence of information which has reached it from the sense organs. The states of the mind which produce that behaviour are its desires, volitions and so forth, and the states of it which modify that behaviour as a result of the influence of the environment are its perceptions, memories and beliefs about the world around it.

In the light of this the materialist thinks he can counter the Cartesian argumentation along the lines I indicated. He also thinks he can counter another objection often made to the identification of the mind with the brain, namely that people knew that they had minds before they knew that they had brains, and that some people have come to dualist views about mind and body. To all this the materialist says that when we talk about the mind and its states we are simply talking about something, of whose real nature and even location, if it has one, we may know little or nothing, which has certain effects upon the organism and is affected by it in certain ways. That something, so far as the mere description of it as mind goes, might be the heart rather than the brain, or might be something mysterious not filling out a position in space at all. However, all modern knowledge points towards the view that what it really is is the brain.

42

The reader must judge this theory for himself, following up the elaborate advocacies and criticisms of it in philosophic literature if he will. For myself I must say I think it misses the real force of the Cartesian argument.

It will be recalled that the Cartesian, as I presented his case, said that it is logically conceivable that whatever an organism does, and whatever is going on inside it physically, it might be an unconscious zombie, lacking mind in the really pregnant sense of consciousness. The materialist must deny this. He must hold that if there is a natural or artificial something inside an organism or robot which makes it behave so as to bring about certain results, regardless of how circumstances, within wide limits, vary, and does so under the control of physical stimuli reaching it from outside, then it has a conscious mind, not as a matter of likely hypothesis but as following from the very meaning of the words 'mind' and 'consciousness'. He must also, I think, say that the idea of a purely solipsistic mind enclosed within the circle of its own ideas is meaningless. But most strikingly of all, he can give no adequate account of what seems to be a necessity for the activity of a genuinely conscious mind, that it has a kind of self-illuminating quality. For the wise Cartesian the self-illuminating quality does not mean that the mind has complete self-knowledge, in the sense that it completely diagnoses all its motives, but it is such that it has a kind of non-conceptual intuitive awareness of what it is about at any time, however little it can think it out explicitly. It may be said that this is true only of conscious mind, but then, as I have said, it is really only conscious mind that the dualist insists stands apart from the physical world as an essentially different sort of thing.

It is of this self-illuminating nature of consciousness that the materialist, as the Cartesian sees it, shows himself to have no grasp. Of course he tries to deal with it in his theorizing, and seeks to explain it as the monitoring of one pattern of brain activity by another. But this is something which might go on in an unconscious zombie or machine. That he simply bypasses in his philosophical thinking that distinctive nature of consciousness, of which in fact he must have his own intuitive sense, becomes particularly clear when he suggests that, of course, dualism might have been true, it might have been that behaviour was controlled by a non-physical entity instead of the brain, it is only that this hypothesis is implausible in the light of modern knowledge. Evidently he has no conception of what this non-physical something might have been, but conceives it as a mere negation. If he formed a positive concept of it he would have found it in himself. In fact, his whole conception of the non-physical mind which he rejects is essentially a materialist one. He thinks of it as a kind of object, whereas the consciousness which, for the Cartesian, is essentially non-physical is not anything which might be discovered, so to speak, in the world but something of which each knows by the lighting up of itself by itself within himself, and of the presence of which in others he finds sufficient intimation to satisfy him.

I turn now to a difficulty for materialists which has received a good deal of doubtfully effective treatment at their hands. It concerns what are called secondary qualities, these being qualities which physical objects present themselves as having to our perception but which seem to vanish on the scientific account of what a physical thing really is, in contrast to the primary qualities, such as shape, mass, and motion, of which, on the face of it, science does not seek to deprive them. The main so-called secondary qualities are colours, smells, tastes, sounds, and warmth and coolness in the character in which we immediately feel them. On the scientific account noise becomes waves in the atmosphere or some other medium, colour a frequency of light waves, warmth a particular motion of molecules and so forth, all of them patterns of movement, or structures, with a minute articulation which seems to clash with the smooth homogeneity of some single such quality as it spreads itself over some portion of space as it seems to us, and lacking in the peculiar 'tang' which makes each quality what it is for us. And such questions arise as whether colour as we experience it can be spread over the surface of an object which is really made up of lots of minute particles separated by spaces larger than themselves. Even if, as is certainly no part of normal scientific notions, the particles were themselves coloured, the colour of the surface as a whole could not be the continuous colour we see it as possessing. Yet the secondary qualities we immediately experience are evidently somehow a part of reality. The dualist normally says that they are really simply aspects of the mind's own internal being, and are thus modes of mind, not really physical at all. Certain idealists say that they do belong to what we may reasonably call the real physical world, because this only exists as something of which we are conscious, and is what we are conscious of it as being, scientific theory only supplying a kind of conceptual tool for dealing with the world given in our experience, not an account of something which really exists. Some emergent materialists hold that somehow these qualities are really spread out in physical space, brought into existence by, but distinct from, the atomic constitutions of things of which science gives the account. Yet it is hard to see how both can fit together in the same part of space. The standard materialist, at least, does not much like this answer. Nor can he put these qualities in the mind as the dualist does, since the mind is the brain and it is as difficult to fit these qualities there as in the physical world around us.

One solution which has been offered is that after all there is no such ineffable tang about each distinct secondary quality such as there is usually said to be. Rather, we simply know that when we sort things out according to their colour, to take this as the simplest example, there is something about these objects which acts on us differently and prompts our putting them in different groups. We cannot say, and do not, in the absence of special scientific information, know, what it is about the objects which affects us differently or what this different effect is. Eventually, however, scientists make this clear by describing how different surfaces in virtue of their minute physical structure reflect light waves of different frequency, thus affecting our eyes and brains differently. The colours then really are either these minute physical structural properties of the surface, or the effects in our brain – materialists diverge as to which. Similar remarks are made about the other secondary qualities.

It seems to me personally that with whatever ingenuity this type of answer is developed it will always remain simply hopeless. Colours, smells, and sounds, in the sense in which they pose this puzzle, are as clearly present to our consciousness as anything can be, each in its distinctive nature, and they cannot turn out to be in their own selves something other than what they seem to be. Obviously a standard materialist writing a book of the present sort would report on matters differently, but in discussing this theory of existence I cannot describe what I think it says without pointing out what seems to me the dead end it reaches. This is not to say that some theory someone may like to call 'materialism' is beyond rescue, but I can see little hope for standard materialism except in the sense that something about the spirit of our times encourages people to swallow it.

Returning now to more detached exposition, a word may be said as to what positive support in favour of his case the standard materialist offers. For so far we have, in fact, considered mainly his attempts to show that certain arguments against it, or in favour of dualism, are not compelling. That only shows, as he is happy to acknowledge, that standard materialism may be true, not that it is.

The line taken by standard materialists is typically this. Once we remove various apparent objections to standard materialism, it will stand forth, certainly not as something proven true, but as the most promising hypothesis for one who has some sense of the manner in which more and more phenomena yield themselves to physical explanation. That there is no knock-down proof in favour of it will even be thought a merit by many, for modern theorists of knowledge usually hold that the attempt to prove by sheer abstract thinking what the essential nature of reality is rests on an unrealistic assessment of the capacity of the human mind and of the kind of support of which any serious proposition about how things are is capable. It may be urged, as a development of this point, that the only kind of purported knowledge which really seems to grow in any steady fashion till it converges on conclusions accepted by all serious persons is scientific knowledge, standing in contrast here to religion and metaphysics. Therefore a view of the nature of things which takes as genuinely existent only the sort of thing with which science deals is allied to the only really reliable kind of theorizing which there is. Of course, there are replies to this, such as that convergence of many on a point of view is not the one mark of truth, and that it is doubtful whether science itself as a human activity is explicable materialistically. Some would also add that the extent to which science has this converging quality is much exaggerated, though frankly I myself think the materialist does have something of a point here.

Actually, speaking from a non-materialist point of view, I think there is an explanation of the appeal of materialism of a different sort, lying in a feature of the human mind which, wrongly understood, makes material-ism look almost self-evident. This lies in the fact that the whole direction of our consciousness in daily life, and presumably of the consciousness of our ancestors among the animals, is concentrated on the things which lie in the space around us to such an extent that our very language tends strongly to equation of real existence with being in a place. If our only objection to materialism is that there are more things in heaven and earth than are dreamt of in that philosophy, and we think of heaven as a place like earth, taking 'in' literally, the things of whose neglect we complain are really physical in their essence, however far from the natural phenomena of science. It is often difficult to get people to realize that the non-physical mind of which Cartesians speak is not, as some have thought it, 'a ghost in the machine' of the human body, since ghosts and 'spirits' such as might appear in a seance are, in contrast to it, as physical, if made of finer stuff, as our ordinary bodies. When we speak of the mental we do so mostly or entirely in metaphors (more or less sleeping) of a physical kind; we *grasp* ideas and have thoughts *in* our minds. Whatever the real source of this materialism which is endemic to most of our thinking, it is not surprising that there should be a theory of existence which follows its leadings. As thinkers we are subjects, but the natural object of thought is objects and it is only with effort that the subject turns its thoughts upon its own un-object-like nature. Such at least is the dualist's likely interpretation of the blandishments of materialism; the materialist himself will think he is only turning from philosophic dreams to the bedrock of common sense, as revised by modern science.

Another attraction of materialism for many lies, I think, in the surely false belief that it is the only properly naturalistic philosophy. But one may reject any notion that there is anything properly called supernatural intervention in the world, without becoming a materialist, certainly a standard materialist. Even if dualism is traditionally associated with belief in a God who stands outside nature, one could hold that mind is something non physical which comes upon the stage when physical nature generates, by way of physical laws, beings of a certain degree of physical complexity. Such a dualism is rather close to emergent materialism, except that the fresh reality of mind is not physical, not spread out in space, as it would have to be for the emergent materialist. The epiphenomenalist dualism of thinkers such as Santayana is essentially naturalistic, while not in a proper sense materialist (though Santayana rather confusingly called his naturalism materialism). It is difficult to say precisely what makes a theory of existence naturalistic, but it would normally imply atheism, denial of immortality and, at least since the nineteenth century, commitment to the view that man arose like other animals in the course of evolution, and has no special source or destiny beyond this world. If one is strongly committed to a naturalism with these ingredients it is a mistake to think it is necessarily at risk if standard materialism, or even emergent materialism, cannot make out its case.

If we ask why people often dislike materialism, rather than why others like it, the answer may be that they think of it as deterministic, and denying human freedom. They are right, of course, to suppose that materialism rules out the existence of some power of self-determination in man which takes him out of the realm of sheer physical law, for though materialism does not strictly imply absolute determinism, according to which everything that will happen is precisely settled by prior physical conditions, the only failure in such settlement allowed turns on an element of sheer randomness which there may be at the heart of physical nature, and even if such randomness can pile up so that what happens in the human brain is not absolutely determined in advance, it is absurd to identify such randomness with freedom. However, not only materialists, but many other philosophers, hold that freedom in any worthwhile sense is compatible with determinism, since one is free to the extent that what one does is affected by adequately informed decision-making, and if decision-making is a process in the brain, as the materialist holds it is, then it is certainly allowed efficacy. The fact that the decision-making is itself physically determined in its upshot does not mean that it was not an essential link in the chain of events. Whether this is an adequate account of freedom is much debated, but one can only decide how materialism stands to human freedom when one has become clear what meaning should be given to that most difficult of words. The materialist himself claims that at least he does better by freedom than the dualist epiphenomenalist.

So much for the account the materialist gives of mind. If it is successful, the task of reducing everything else with any kind of concrete existence to the physical should not be too difficult. Each of the following sorts of thing is thought by some to have a non-physical aspect to its being: nations, works of art of various kinds, traditions, languages, values. Regarding these, granted that somehow he has done justice to mind, the materialist's problems are much the same as the dualist's. Both would agree that a nation is a group of human beings organized in a certain way and with a certain feeling of affinity to each other common among them. For the materialist the feeling and the behaviour here would be physical states of certain physical organisms, and neither he nor the usual kind of dualist would think there was anything more to the existence of the group of persons than the people and certain relations which link them. Works of art for the materialist would be physical objects or occurrences to which human beings respond in certain ultimately physical ways, while traditions would be habits of behaviour passed on by habits of imitation (the fact that organisms imitate each other being a physical fact explicable in terms of the workings of the brain). A language would be a complex system of behaviours by which groups of human organisms affect those brain processes which are their thoughts. The materialist is no more obliged than any other theorist of existence to be ready with answers to the innumerable problems there are as to how these systems of behaviours developed and are sustained, but only needs to dismiss reasons given for saying that the explanation must be non-physical. Evidently these problems are in the last resort further problems as to the nature of the human mind. The modern materialist usually looks hopefully to the developments of research in the field of artificial intelligence, in which mechanisms, in which it is clear no non-physical factor is at work, are designed to simulate human behaviours so far as possible. The interactionist dualist will be surprised if there do not turn out to be only quite narrow limits within which this can succeed, and so far as it does so he will probably look on the artificial intelligences as zombies such as we have mentioned already. (The epiphenomenalist dualist may think that some actually do have non-physical consciousnesses. The fact that it would be difficult to know whether they really did have conscious minds, a difficulty after all encountered in relation to certain animals, say insects, will be thought of as supporting, not threatening, his kind of dualism, for which conscious mind is a reality, distinct from the physical, the existence of which cannot be definitively settled from outside.)

As to the nature of values, there are many theories on the matter and several of them are open to a materialist. Probably the view which suits him best is the view that what a person or society calls their values are goals to the pursuit of which they are committed with a certain special depth of feeling, this commitment arising from a mixture of social conditioning, genetically determined drives which have been favoured by natural selection, and perhaps realistic insight into what is and what is not attainable in human life. I shall conclude this chapter with a brief sketch of the actual values which have been most associated with materialism and which seem most naturally to fit it.

The great ancient materialists, in particular Epicurus and his Roman follower Lucretius, held that most human suffering came from restlessly striving for more than one really needs. Therefore the wisest course is to learn to be content with the various ordinary satisfactions of daily life and to cope with the ever-present problems of anxiety by bringing home to oneself the irrationality of its usual sources. Of these the main one is the fear of death, based on the sense that some unknown and perhaps horrible fate lies in the hereafter, or in a kind of misinterpretation of the nothingness of extinction as some alarming state of being. Once fully realize that death is no evil lying in wait for one, because while one is, death is not, and when death is, one is not – for the physical nature of mind means that it certainly ceases when physical life is over – and the main source of anxiety will be stilled, and one can devote oneself calmly to cultivating the pleasures careful reflection shows to be the most rewarding, of which the chief is friendship. For Epicurus, as for most subsequent materialists, all positive values are pleasures, all negative ones forms of suffering, but pleasure is best maximized by developing habits of quiet contentment, not by frenetic jollifications.

A modern exponent of a philosophy of life quite close to that of Epicurus is Bertrand Russell. Although his philosophy was not materialist without qualification, it came close to materialism, and his attitude to life was one typical of materialists.

In his book *The Conquest of Happiness* Russell reflects on how to live a happy life in a manner with a definite continuity with Epicureanism. However, Russell, as is well known, was a man of strong social concern, and was thereby committed to an ethic according to which each should do his best to advance the greatest happiness of the greatest number of human beings, and indeed of animals, not, indeed, neglecting a wise care for one's own happiness as that most immediately under one's own control. This is the so-called utilitarian doctrine of Jeremy Bentham (1748–1832), whose own theory of existence approximated to materialism.

How does this view of values and of morality relate to the 'washing-machine' materialism mentioned at the beginning of this chapter? Certainly if the latter term was taken to imply concern especially with washing-machines and colour television for oneself alone, the two are poles apart. Utilitarianism is most high-minded in the amount of concern with the welfare of others it demands of each. If, however, it is taken as implying a certain vision of the good society, there is some affinity. The utilitarian is set on the goal of people in general having just the kind of life, including possessions, they will like most, not the kind of life they ought to like, according to some *ought* arising from some transcendent sphere. That will almost certainly mean a strong emphasis upon the wide availability of labour-saving devices and pleasant entertainment. On the other hand, it need imply no devaluation of high culture, contemplation, and intellectual endeavour not merely geared to improving man's comfort, if these actually prove themselves in experience as giving people the most satisfying lives. So utilitarianism is against any moralistic condemnation of pleasures (pornography might be an example) which is not based on real insight into their deleterious consequences, and to that rather limited extent does approximate to materialism in the popular sense.

Why should the materialist typically incline to some kind of utilitarianism? An explanation, if not a justification, is this. The materialist is typically motivated by a hostility to anything he thinks of as an airy-fairy invention which he suspects has been concocted to flatter human vanity or cater for a love of mystery. He thinks that a non-physical mind or soul, capable of surviving death, is something of this sort, and thinks likewise of non-materialist accounts of works of art and their genesis and other such things. He wants to stick to the palpable facts acknowledged by everyone in daily life, avoiding all idle or superstitious fancies. Science, of course, adds to the facts which confront us all, but not by moving towards a different realm entirely. The same feelings inspire his valuations. Pleasure and pain are matters of obvious fact, not affairs of vague speculation. Other values, in so far as they cannot be reduced to this, such as beauty thought of as something other than a pleasant sensation, or a virtuous disposition other than as habits which make oneself or others happy, are quite remote from anything the human animal can expect to bump upon or feel in the same direct fashion. Above all, the materialist prides himself upon not being taken in by vaguely uplifting language, and on adopting a thoroughly realistic view of things. Utilitarianism, at least in its naïver forms, caters for this kind of mind. It sets up as the goal of human endeavour something which it is presumed that everyone is after in any case, and does not attempt to deflect men from their natural goals by mystification.

The suggestion that pleasure is the natural goal of man, with pain the one thing he naturally seeks to avoid, is not beyond challenge, from a biological or ethological point of view, and some materialists would see the best way of building an ethic on man's actual physical biological being to lie in a determination of the behaviour patterns which are somehow appropriate to him as a species and contribute most to his survival, and in setting these up as norms against variations which threaten the species. But on the whole utilitarianism has been the materialist's ethical creed.

Yet there are two ways in which it has been thought that materialists are in difficulties in making sense of a utilitarian (or perhaps any other) morality. Of these the first, I think, is no real problem for them. It concerns the rationale a materialist can offer for the demand upon the individual that he concern himself with the welfare of others and not solely with his own. To this the brief answer is that if, as was suggested above, one's values are the goals to which one is most deeply committed, there is no reason why the materialist should not find himself deeply committed to the general welfare, and find a corresponding commitment as arousable in others when the needs of humanity in general are brought home to them. (That natural selection should have favoured a concern with other members of one's species, with a concern with other species perhaps as a spill-off effect from this, has seemed intelligible, for though the altruist might not survive to breed himself, a society lacking a pool of genes producing altruism would be at serious risk. There are, however, certain problems which socio-biologists see in genes for altruism, wich complicate the picture.)

The second difficulty is much more serious, though it is only a case, as, to be blunt, I see it, of the essential absurdity of materialism. If pain is only a certain pattern of electrical stimulation going on in the brain, producing movements of retreat from a stimulus on the part of an organism, and pleasure something similar producing movement towards, why should it matter two figs how much there is of one or the other? Imagine one had the power, so to speak, to *see* these goings on in detail while also grasping the larger-scale patterns thus constituted. Would one see anything which explained why the excitation called pain, or the associated large-scale movements of the organism, was something especially to be prevented? Similarly, contrariwise, for pleasure. Surely not, even if the patterns had some prettiness or otherwise (itself, for the materialist, a matter of patterns produced in response to them in one's own brain). I have had to put the matter crudely, for the sake of brevity, but no amount of sophistication in the way of putting it would alter the essential point. The materialist may say that it is no easier to *prove* the desirability of pleasure and undesirability of pain on the dualist account. But that is not the point. Prove it or not, when one imagines pleasure or pain one imagines something which, in fact, solicits one's concern, but what one then imagines simply drops out of reality on the materialist view. It was partly realization of such points which led thinkers such as Russell and Bentham to qualify their materialism in ways not for exploration here.

I shall conclude with a brief word about the dialectical materialism advocated by Karl Marx and Engels and by subsequent Marxists.

Dialectical materialism is derived from the non-materialist idealist philosophy of Hegel. From the Hegelian point of view, the whole of reality represents the coming into consciousness of its own being of a kind of cosmic spirit, referred to as the Absolute Idea. There are three levels of being within the structure of the Absolute Idea. At the first level it is a system of abstract concepts, somewhat akin to the forms of Plato, and thus not simply the terms in which minds think about the world but the basic forms of being of which anything that actually exists must be the more or less successful actualization. These concepts belong in a series in which each corrects the inadequacy of its predecessor. To learn to understand how one of these concepts points to the next one in the series is to learn to think dialectically, and the series itself is what is called a dialectic series. One way in which the concepts may follow on from one another is that there is a certain clash between elements held together within one concept, so that each element seems both to demand and to repel the other, and the next concept in the series unites those same elements in a more coherent manner, and somehow even *is* the prior concept in an improved version of itself. The second level of being within the total structure of the Absolute Idea is physical nature. This is a continuation of the dialectic line of concepts in which each concept remedies defects in its predecessor, but the concepts here are not mere abstractions but forms realized in concrete natural phenomena – moreover, the concepts realized in nature are more determinate versions of the less rich among the abstract concepts of the first level. In consequence of this, everything in physical nature has a kind of tension within itself which is resolved in some other physical phenomenon. Hegel does not think of these different physical phenomena as following on each other chronologically, but the theory very much lends itself, especially in the light of scientific developments since Hegel, to a modification which makes it so, and, in particular, sees the development of organic life as passing through phases which follow on from each other in dialectic fashion.

We now come to the third level of being within the structure of the Absolute Idea, which is the realm of conscious mind as found in human beings. As actualized in physical nature the Absolute Idea is said to be alienated from itself, because the relations between physical phenomena do not do justice to the way in which the sequence of concepts is something which of itself demands to be grasped in thought. When human beings come on the scene the sequence of concepts in the dialectic series actualizes itself in a series of different ways in which human beings think about themselves, and about the world they live in, and thus in a series of ways in which they organize themselves socially and individually in the light of these successive types of thought. Here there definitely is a chronological development along the dialectic line, though it does not always stick precisely to the series of the pure concepts, because one of the concepts which has to actualize itself is the concept of contingency or irrationality. But by and large the development of human modes of life and organization is the progress of human thinking along the dialectic line.

Does the line have an ending, it may be asked, for it does, it seems, have a beginning in the concept of *pure being*, reflected in the fact that the earliest human thought is just a blank grasp that things are? The answer is affirmative, for the final concept is a concept which sums up the whole of the previous series and exhibits the manner and details of its development. This final concept, which is in a certain sense the Absolute Idea itself brought to a final focus, is actualized in men like Hegel who understand the universe for what it is.

Marx and Engels took over from Hegel the idea that phenomena in nature, and in human life and organization, each contain a kind of clash of elements which is resolved in another phenomenon which, however, in virtue of its own internal clashes, points towards another phenomenon which resolves these, and so forth. In human life at least the sequence is, as with Hegel, thought of as being chronological and as supplying the motive power of historical development. In physical nature, I understand, there are both chronological and non-chronological such dialectical transitions.

However, the dialectical vision of reality held by these two thinkers is materialistic not idealistic, because first, the dialectical nature of things is built into nature and man without reflecting the urge to self-expression of any cosmic spirit, and secondly, the development of human history, through dialectic transitions, is not so much a matter of ways of thinking as that of forms of social organization based on the modes of production dominant in a human society at any time. So in explaining human history, and even human theorizing, dialectically, we should study how one means of production and associated social organization contained conflicts within it, that is actual human antagonisms, which could only be resolved by passage to another such means of production and social organization which, however, would have its own internal clashes eventually forcing a further dialectical development. In terms of this general outlook Marx and Engels interpreted human history as leading up to the capitalist society of their day, and as pointing on beyond it to what is sometimes called a socialist society, in which the dictatorship of the proletariat would hold. Eventually this would pass on dialectically to a state of communism proper, at which point the character of further developments would be a matter for the free decision of mankind in a way which had never held before.

Something like half the world is under communist governments for which Marxism is the orthodoxy, officially, though most intellectual Marxists would claim they are not truly Marxist in their behaviour. I shall not attempt to sketch the Marxist political or ethical outlook, since the person who wishes to learn about it will find no lack of better guides. As regards what in the end constitutes a satisfactory life for a human being, it is doubtful whether Marxists have anything that unique to say. It is a life of something like complete fulfilment of the individual's potentialities of a sort which it is said people in general could only have in a communist society.

It is rather doubtful how far dialectical materialism is, or in order to preserve its main theses needs to be, materialist in the strict sense of holding that all genuine realities are physical. What it does hold, certainly, is that the basis of the dialectical development of human history is powered by transitions of a necessary kind from one way of organizing the production of the goods required in human life to another, and not primarily by the influence of human theorizing carried out independently of economic conditions, and that therefore, until perhaps the future communist society develops, it is man's ways of organizing physical work which are the mainspring of development. It also, of course, denies that there is any spiritual source of the world, and insists that physical reality is the ultimate source and background of all that is. It is quite proper to call this theory materialist in a general sense, but it does not really preclude the rejection of the strong materialistic thesis that there are no realities which are not physical.

[THREE]

IDEALISM

Just as materialism drops mind as a reality genuinely distinct from the physical, so does idealism drop the physical as something which exists other than as an aspect of mind's own being. There are very many great idealist thinkers. Those whom I shall mainly consider are George Berkeley (1685–1753), Immanuel Kant (1724–1804), and F. H. Bradley (1846–1924). We touched on Hegel (1770–1831) towards the end of the last chapter. He is one of the most influential of philosophers, and is usually regarded as an idealist, but this is in a sense somewhat different from that in which we shall be understanding the expression, and in any case I would not know how to deal with his philosophy with any seriousness except at a length impossible here.

Berkeley's brilliantly argued philosophy arose initially as a reaction against the philosophy of John Locke (1632–1704), which is essentially dualistic. For Locke, we know of the existence of physical things only through images which occur in our minds as a result of events in the brain which have been caused, via our sense organs, by things in the physical world of which these images give us a conception in some ways substantially correct, in some ways misleading. The real physical things have shapes and move about, for example, in a way of which the characteristics of our images give us a fair conception on the whole – though it blurs the finer details – but the colours, smells and noises and so forth which are found in the image world of which alone we are directly conscious do not exist in the real physical world. These are the secondary qualities of which we have already spoken.

The word Locke actually uses to put forward his view is 'ideas' not 'images', but the exposition of both Locke's and Berkeley's thought is likely to be much less confusing if we use the latter word. It must be clear, however, that the images of which we speak are not solely visual. Quite apart from present issues, it is convenient to say that when one imagines a sound or the feel of something one has an auditory or a tactile image. The Lockean proposal is that when one sees things, hears sounds, or feels things it is always only visual, auditory or tactile images that one experiences directly, though these prompt one to believe in a real physical thing or occurrence which causes these images to spring up in one's mind and to which they somehow correspond. The reason for this view is essentially the Cartesian one, namely that by reflection on the possibility that life is after all a kind of dream one realizes that there is no necessary connection between the existence of that which undeniably confronts one as an aspect of one's own experience in perception, and a real physical thing spread out in space.

Berkeley argued that if all one ever directly experiences in perception is images in one's own mind, one can never have had an opportunity to learn that their occurrence is correlated with the existence of any real thing beyond. So if by physical things we mean something thus lying beyond our own experience, or that of any other mind with whom we can communicate, there is no reason to believe that they are really there at all. But that does not mean that we should doubt that tables, trees and water exist, or even our own bodies, for what we really mean by these things are those groups of images which the Cartesian speaks of as only being caused by real things. That is what ordinary people mean, when they speak of ordinary things, else they would not feel so sure that seeing, touching and so forth is believing. Not that common sense quite recognizes that the thing one calls a table, or even one's own body, is simply a group of images. Since they are images (or ideas) they can only exist as aspects of the experience of a mind; they cannot really exist when not perceived. This is not merely because the philosopher has chosen to call them 'images' or 'ideas' but follows from reflection on the nature of that with which we are directly acquainted in perceptual experience. For example, the objects we immediately experience always have a certain perspectival character which alters according to where we perceive them from. (Perspective must be taken in an extended sense, when senses other than sight are concerned, to refer to the change in what we experience according to the relation we stand in to objects when perceiving them, as for instance the precise sort of movements by which we touch a thing, or where we smell it from.) Also they are always qualified as somehow pleasant or unpleasant, and this 'hedonic quality' is not something besides the object we are perceiving, but an element in its very being – intense heat, for example, is not accompanied by pain, but *is* a pain, and beautiful colours are pleasures, not things which cause pleasure. Since all would grant that pleasure and pain cannot exist except as aspects of a mind's experience, it follows that what we are immediately aware of when we perceive things can only exist as aspects of the mind's own being, and are therefore properly called images or ideas. As we have seen, Berkeley thought we had no justification for postulating so-called real things somehow back of these images. Moreover, since these supposed real things are conceived on the model of our images, they would be simply things of the same kind and would equally only be capable of existing as aspects of the being of some mind. It is little use trying, as Locke and Descartes did, to specify the real things as somehow lacking everything which marks our images as mind-dependent, such as colour, which they all agreed could only exist within a mind, or hedonic and perspectival qualities. Try seriously to remove these features from one's conception of a physical thing and one is left trying to imagine a mere blank. How could there be a shape without something like a colour to fill up the space of which it is the outline?

Thus, though by more thorough argumentation, did Berkeley set out to defend his theory of existence, the first fully idealist one in Western thought, according to which the only genuinely existing physical world is a system of images which has no existence except as an aspect of the being of the many minds which make up the real stuffing – to use a word misleading if taken in any literal fashion – of the world. His arguments are very powerful indeed, but they leave the obvious question: What explains the fact that our images come and go in such an orderly fashion (partly in response to the way in which we make the images which constitute our body move about within our image 'fields', according to that power of controlling them which we find we have) that there is a strong temptation to think that they are really there with an independent existence even when it seems that no mind is perceiving them? Before looking at Berkeley's answer, let us make clear to ourselves that so far as the minds which experience all this imagery go Berkeley's view is essentially the Cartesian one. A mind is not an image or collection of images, it is that which experiences images and finds powers of willing and thinking in itself. We cannot imagine a mind, but we know what a mind is by our direct experience of being one.

Berkeley held that, indeed, we have good reason to suppose that the physical world exists still in some sense even when no mind like our own experiences it. He argued that this could only be explained as resting on the existence of an infinite spirit, in short God, who has given himself a vast system of imagery which he uses as a cue on the basis of which he decides to provide minds like us with images duplicating part of that system. As finite minds we have control, subject to God's assent, of the images we call our bodies, and the use we make of this control settles the particular path through God's imagery of which he will give us a duplication.

It may be objected that if Berkeley thinks we have grounds for supposing that there is a vast system of images in a divine mind of which our images are the duplication, he seems to employ much the same kind of reasoning which he condemned in Locke. His reply, roughly, is that Locke thought that from the existence of a certain regularity in our imagery we could infer the existence of something which was not supposed to be imagery at all, and which, moreover, was something of which we could form nothing but incoherent conceptions, since we have to imagine something lacking all the qualities which mark our images as mind-dependent. In the case of God, and his imagery, the matter is quite different. God is a mind we conceive as an infinitely more glorious thing of the sort we experience ourselves as being, and his imagery is likewise something of the same essential category as our own.

There are many philosophers who go a long way with Berkeley, in holding that the only physical world of which we know is that whose existence is one with a certain orderliness in the imagery we experience, but who deny that this gives any ground for postulating a God. It is just a brute fact that as well as the images we do experience there are definite other images available to us if we take the right steps. The physical world, in so far as it is not perceived by anyone, exists only in the sense that there are definite truths as to what images are available to minds. These philosophers are sometimes called phenomenalists, though the term is sometimes reserved for those who deny that there is any active mind at all which has the images, and reduce both mind and physical world to a kind of vortex of imagery existing nowhere. Such philosophers, also called 'sensationalists', since only sensations or images have existence for them, are not usually regarded as idealists at all. Since the world, according to them, is simply a kind of buzzing of senseless sensation, the general spirit of their doctrine comes rather close to that of materialism, different as is their ultimate conception of the world.

Kant developed a version of idealism, much more complex than Berkeley's, but also closer to it in its main theses than he seems to have realized. He called it transcendental idealism, contrasting it with what he called empirical idealism which merely said that the physical world does not, or does not certainly, exist. For the transcendental idealist the physical world certainly does exist, but it exists only as a system of possible appearances for minds. What distinguishes Kant's idealism from Berkeley's is mainly that he gave a much more positive role to our minds in determining the kind of world we experience. The fact that everything we come across in what we call the real world exists in space and time is because our mind is so constructed that both our perceptual experience and all our thinking present objects in spatial and temporal guise. That the spatial and temporal character of the physical world as we experience it is not something pertaining to any independently existing reality, but stems rather from our particular way of cognizing things, is attested, according to Kant, by the fact that we can settle on the essential character of space (as, for example, excluding parallel lines from meeting) and of time, merely by exploring our own capacity or otherwise to imagine certain things without any need to resort to observation or experiment. Surely we could not thus discover the essential traits of space and time merely by tapping the resources of our own mind, unless they are really patterns, contained within itself, which it somehow so imposes upon the reality, in the midst of which it exists, that it does not know what on earth it can be like in its own bare being.

The details of Kant's argumentation in this connection have become outmoded with the development and scientific application of non-Euclidean geometries, and other shifts in science, but a good case can still be made out for his main thesis that the pervasive characteristics of the world of ordinary experience reflect more our own way of experiencing the world than its inherent nature.

So Kant did not deny that there is a real world independent of our minds. When I shift my position and see different things this must be because I have altered the relations in which I stand to the constituents of some kind of real world. Since, for him, then, the world of familiar experience arises from the interaction between my mind and these unimaginable real things, Kant sees no need to appeal, like Berkeley, to a God in whose imagery we participate. But we must avoid assimilating his position to that of a realist about the physical world like Locke, and taking these unimaginable things in themselves as physical realities which act upon our sense organs, for they have no physical properties such as shape and movement, while our sense organs themselves are only features of that show world which arises from the action of the things in themselves upon our minds. So Kant comes close to Berkeley in holding that physical things are a kind of system of appearances existing only in our minds. As for the things no one is perceiving, they are what would come into being as objects of our awareness if we moved our bodies about in the show world in ways which would somehow set us in relation to other aspects of the realm of things in themselves, the noumenal world as it is also called.

Thus the physical only has being as an aspect of mind. Here Kant is at one with Berkeley. However, unlike Berkeley, Kant's position forces him to make of our mind itself something mysterious not revealed to us in its own true being. For it is something about its hidden depths which gives it that spatializing and temporalizing character, through which it converts everything else with which it comes into contact into something with spatial and temporal properties which, in its own true being, it lacks. Thus Kant thought that there are not only things in themselves which are what physical objects really are, but also things in themselves which are what our minds really are. One feature of this doctrine which appealed to him was that he thought our minds as they really are might possess true freedom, even if our minds as they appear belong together with the physical world in a deterministic causal nexus. Anyone sympathetic to Cartesianism will hold that Kant here loses sight of the essential character of mind as something self-illuminating just as the materialist does, and that some mysterious thing in itself can no more be that individual consciousness which I experience myself as being than can my brain. Thus even if the thing in itself which is my noumenal ego, the thing in itself I truly am, is somehow free, that does not make me free, but at most the puppet of some mysterious other's freedom. However, there are many today of a Kantian persuasion who accept Kant's claim that, by exhibiting the physical world and our minds as known to us as belonging to a show world, he showed how it might be possible that the true world of things in themselves might be one answering to the aspirations of religious faith, for though Kant rejected any Berkeleyan (or Cartesian) proof of God's existence, he did think that his philosophy, by its contrast between the unknown real world, and the show or phenomenal world of daily life, removed any ground for rejecting religious faith as falsifiable by facts about the present world.

This whole Kantian viewpoint can be pushed in a somewhat different direction from this, in which, as I see it, it becomes much more persuasive. The philosopher who has especially pointed the way to this is Schopenhauer, whose theory of existence we shall consider in a later chapter. I wish now to turn to a third kind of idealism, known as absolute idealism. This exists in many more or less different versions. My account will largely follow Bradley.

It is a leading principle of absolute idealism that sentient experience, and what exists only as an element therein, is all that there really is or could be. Bradley put it thus: 'We perceive, on reflection, that to be real or even barely to exist, must be to fall within sentience. Sentient experience, in short, is reality, and what is not this is not real. We may say, in other words, that there is no being or fact outside of that which is commonly called psychical existence. Feeling, thought, and volition (any groups under which we class psychical phenomena) are all the materials of existence, and there is no other material, actual or even possible.' (*Appearance and Reality* by F. H. Bradley, Chapter XIV.)

Bradley is appealing to us to make a thought experiment in which we try to bring home to ourselves in a fashion which goes beyond the mere mouthing of words what we really have in mind when we think of anything as existing, and claims that either the object of our thought will become a mere blank or will present itself as some kind of mental activity or content of experience. If you try to think of what you are really believing in when you believe in the existence of a friend, whom you think of as engaged in some particular activity what you actually have in mind is either the experiences he is having or the experiences someone may be having in observing him. If no one actually is observing him, then you will have to admit that what you are thinking of as existing in the second case is not actual, but only what would exist if he were, as we say, observed. If you try to form a clear conception of what an inanimate thing like a house is, there is nothing you can bring clearly to mind except the experiences people do or might have if they perceived the house in some way, or gave themselves the experiences they would get in carrying out repairs on it, and so forth. Here again, unless someone actually has these experiences, what you are thinking of is only something which past experience advises you might be brought into existence. In a rather different way, if one asks what *numbers* are, you can only really bring their nature home to yourself by imagining activities of mathematical calculation, and so forth.

The idea is not necessarily that physical things and numbers are themselves experiences or mental activities, but that they are elements in these which cannot be thought of as existing in separation from them. A total experience usually has a subject side and an object side, and houses and numbers belong to the object side of certain experiences. The object side, however, owes its particular character to the kind of subjective activity directed at it in such a way that the notion of an object not belonging together with experience directed at it is the notion of a mere blank.

It is well to be clear that this line of thought does not turn on a fallacious piece of reasoning one sometimes meets with in idealists, but which weakens rather than strengthens their case. Berkeley sometimes seems to suggest that one cannot think of something which is not the object of a mind's experience, since anything you *think of* thereby is an *object of your experience*, and to give this as a reason why it is futile to postulate objects which do not belong to someone's experience. If this argument had anything in it, it would show that one could not coherently believe in anything other than what pertained to one's own personal experience, and since Berkeley certainly believes in the minds of God and other human beings, each with its own ideas, that would refute his own philosophy as much as any other position except that of pure solipsism. The fallacy of this argument is that it confuses what one is thinking about with the activity of thinking about it. It also ignores the fact that one can think of the class of things of a certain type, such as the class of Indonesians, without thinking of any individual member of the class, and can thus think of the class of things one has never thought of. But this thoroughly fallacious argument has nothing to do with the contention under discussion now. Bradley does not deny that you can think of experiences which you are not personally having. True, you have to specify them to yourself in terms drawn from your own experience, you have to have some kind of imagery in your mind which adumbrates the characteristics you are ascribing to something outside your mind. You are, however, projecting these characteristics into the world beyond your own personal experience as something which you believe exists there independently of yourself. This is what happens when I try to imagine someone else's feelings. The claim made is that we have no materials for forming a conception of something which would not pertain to some kind of mental activity or experience.

It is a likely objection to this line of thought that even if there is nothing in our experience from which we can gain a conception of something which does not exist as an element in some experience, that does not show that there may not be some such thing. May there not be un-imaginable things in themselves such as Kant supposed? The Bradleyan will answer that when you say that there may *be* such things, you are simply attaching no meaning to the word 'be'. If you can form no genuine conception in your mind of what this being is, which they are supposed to have, such as goes beyond the mere stringing of words together, then you are not just without any conception of what it is which you think has being, but the very talk of being is the mouthing of an empty word.

You are trying to form a conception of what the philosopher Whitehead, not quite an idealist, but in this point at one with thinkers like Bradley, referred to as 'vacuous reality', a kind of being which is mere blankness. Of course, you can think of a thing while leaving much of its specific nature undetermined in your mind. You can think of grief, or of a picture, without determining its precise nature, or every detail of it, but what happens then is that you have some kind of image in your mind and think of something which answers to certain of its more general characteristics, while regarding it as varying from the image in other detailed ways you leave quite open. The matter is different if there is nothing in your mind which gives any positive indication at all of the character of that of which you are thinking.

One feature of this line of thought is, clearly, that it is insisted that if you really know what you are thinking of, this is because you can form a conception of it which goes beyond mere verbal description. This need not, however, take the form of an 'image' in any at all usual sense. It is only required that there be some materials within your experience from which you can derive a sense of its character. Where you cannot do this at all, the thing you speak of can, at best, be regarded as a kind of verbal fiction serving certain practical purposes. This is how idealists tend to look upon the notion of physical realities which exist in detachment from any kind of experience. Whenever you really bring home to yourself the character you conceive a physical thing as having, you find that this includes characteristics it can only have within an experience. It will be conceived as having a certain aesthetic quality, as perceived from some vaguely suggested point of view, and as organized into a certain kind of 'gestalt', as psychologists call it, namely the kind of thing which changes as you see an ambiguous drawing in different ways, but which is, in fact, present in all perception. You may, indeed, leave it vague in your mind which of these mind-dependent qualities it has, as you leave it vague what colour hair a man has when you treat any colour in your imagery as irrelevant to your thought, but you cannot form a, so to speak, positive conception of what a physical thing would be like denuded of all qualities which reflect a mind's awareness of it, and thus your belief that there may be a physical thing denuded of such qualities is merely a verbal belief in something of which you have no real conception. As for the entities postulated or detected by science at levels below observation, they are characterized in terms too abstract to constitute the whole real being of any genuine entity. They must, therefore, either be simply useful conceptual fictions or possess some unknown further more concrete characteristics, and reflection shows that any such characteristics would have to be, like all qualities of which we know, elements in some sentient experience, even if not in ours.

The absolute idealist, then, rejects the idea that there is anything other than sentient experience and its contents. This does not mean, however, that there is nothing but the experiences of humans, animals, and perhaps God. Some absolute idealists hold that what appears to us as inanimate nature is really some kind of ocean of interacting low-level centres of experience, pulsing with dim emotion, though this is strongly rejected by others who think that the physical world exists only as the main object side of centres of experience like ours. In either case, this latter is what the physical world primarily is *for us*.

We must clarify what is meant by the expression 'centre of experience', which I have just used, on the Bradleyan scheme. One's centre of experience at any given time is not something which has experiences, rather is it the total experience one is living through at any particular moment. It is that which I try to imagine if I try to imagine what it is like being you at this particular moment in just the circumstances you are in. It includes, therefore, not merely your internal feelings and thoughts but the things around you in the room in just that character they have for you at the moment, and even the political situation of the country, if you are thinking of it, in just the manner it presents itself to you. One can either think of there being a series of such centres of experience, each being what it is like being you in your world at successive moments, or think of your centre of experience as a single enduring thing which changes through time.

The self or ego, that which refers to itself as 'I', is not something which *has* the experiences which make up a centre of experience. Rather is it one aspect of the centre which is directed upon that other aspect of it which makes up the centre's object aspect. As I look at the furniture in the room and wonder how to rearrange it, that wondering helps make up the self, while the furniture, as it exists within that centre, is the self's object. If I do rearrange the furniture my voluntary bodily movements become part of the self, but parts of the body which are merely passively there to be observed belong rather to the mere object world. One cannot say that the self has that total experience which is the centre of experience of the moment, because it is as much part of the experience as are the things at which it directs its concerns.

What then does have the experience, what is the true subject? An initial answer is that we must break away from conventional categories, if we are to understand this matter, and say that the centre of experience experiences itself, although the centre as a whole does more especially identify itself with that part of itself which constitutes the self or ego. This is an idea somewhat akin to one which Sartre developed in his work *The Transcendence of the Ego.*

There is a striking divergence here between the Bradleyan sort of absolute idealist, and the other idealists we have considered. In one way or another they distinguish the subject which has the experiences, the mind or spirit, from the experiences which it has. For the Bradleyan, in contrast, experience exists in the form of total units or centres of experience which experience themselves, and do not stand in any contrast to what they feel.

But the Bradleyan stands in quite as important a contrast to the 'sensationalist' philosophy on which I briefly touched above, for which reality consists in a kind of vortex of sensations existing, as I put it, nowhere, since we should not think of them as in space.

The supreme 'sensationalist' philosopher was David Hume (1711–76). He held, or at least often seems to have held, that all that really existed were innumerable individual sensations, images, pulses of feeling, tweaks and tingles which somehow fall into separate groups and sequences, which constitute you, me and other conscious beings, and follow on each other or occur together according to laws partly discoverable. As I have noted, there is a certain similarity in the appeal of sensationalism and materialism, and different as, on the face of it, they are, various thinkers, including sometimes Bertrand Russell, have attempted to combine them.

One of the great difficulties for sensationalism concerns what bundles all your sensations, images, feelings together in one group, and mine in another group, so as to constitute the obvious difference there is between your having a feeling and my doing so. Must there not be some kind of metaphysical glue which binds them together? But that is to appeal to something mysterious in itself, and not readily countenanced by sensationalists. Hume himself admitted the difficulty to be very serious, and was not satisfied that he had found the answer.

Cartesians, Berkeleyans and materialists all have their answers to this question. For the first two, sensations and so forth belong together because there is a single mind which has them, while for the materialist they are physical events in different organisms. The Bradleyan answer is, however, that the very problem is misconceived, for it supposes that there are these distinct items known as sensations, images and feelings, which, separate in themselves, have to be brought together by some external principle. As against this the Bradleyan holds that the individual centre of experience is itself the only genuine item in the case. Each centre, at each moment, is as basic a unit as there is to be found in the universe, and what we call its distinct sensations and so forth are simply semi-fictitious entities the exigencies of language drive us to speak of when we try to describe, so far as it can be captured in words at all, the distinctive character of some one such centre. Certainly that character is in some sense variegated, the centre has different aspects, such as its self and object side, but these different aspects are so shot through with qualification by the precise contrasts they stand in to all other aspects of the centre that they could never occur in quite the same specific character in any other whole of experience, and are simply distinguishable aspects of a whole which is much more a one than a many. Even to speak of it as a whole is misleading, since that tends to suggest that it has separable parts, rather than distinguishable aspects.

This is the Bradleyan answer to the question as to what links all our so-called different experiences together at a particular moment, granted there is no separate mind to have them. By a single moment, here, is not meant some mere instant, but the shortest period in which a change can be taken in as a single totality, as when one actually sees a movement, or hears a phrase of music as a whole. It is less obvious what the Bradleyan answer is to the question as to what links your centre of experience at one moment to the next, but basically it is a matter of a certain special continuity of character.

These centres of experience, then, are at one level the ultimate con-stituents of the universe. All the same, there is something not quite real about their separate individuality. For just as the sensationalist has a problem as to what links distinct sensations, images and feelings together so as to constitute a single mind, so there seems, for the conception we have now reached, a problem as to what links all these centres together in a single universe in which the self pertaining to one centre can com-municate and have anything whatever to do with the self pertaining to another centre. And quite apart from the problem of communication, surely everything in the universe must stand in some relation or other to everything else in the universe. We can only mean, when we talk of the universe, or of that whole of things concerning which one expects a theory of existence to give some account, that system of things to every part of which we stand in some sort of relation, more or less direct. If there were some entity out of all relation to us whatever, such that there was no series of intermediaries, related each to each and leading from us to it, it would be no part of what we call the universe, and, in any case, Bradley offers arguments, which I shall not explore, for saying that such total disconnection between one thing and another is an impossibility

Actually Bradley thinks that, when we come to a proper grasp of things, we will realize that talking of things as standing in *relations* of one sort or another to each other fails to do justice to the ultimate togetherness of everything with everything, since the very idea that they are linked by something called a relation suggests an initial apartness which the relation overcomes. He expresses this in the rather odd assertion that relations are unreal. I shall ignore this point in my exposition of the essential Bradleyan vision of reality, at least so far as my use of words goes, for the main points can be made without the verbal contortions otherwise demanded of us.

The usual way of conceiving the fact that everything is in some relation to everything else is to think of everything as existing in a single space and time. If this were so, there would be some temporal and spatial distance between each pair of things. That way of conceiving the unity of the universe cannot be the literal truth for the Bradleyan. Centres of experience cannot be thought of as existing in space. There is no distance between the house as I see it and the same house as you see it. Space is rather in centres of experience than something they are in. In your centre there is a distance between your body as it figures there and mine, but there is no distance between your body felt in your centre as the core of the universe, and your body as it is for me as something at a sensible distance from the throbbing core of my body. (This again is a Bradleyan theme which is echoed in Sartre.)

But though this usual way of conceiving the togetherness, more or less close, of everything with everything, by way of the notion of a common space and time, is not the metaphysical truth, it serves as an image which brings home to us what is an ultimate truth, that things can only stand in relation to each other when there is a whole, homogeneous in nature with themselves, and in which they are both included. Spatially extended and enduring things are capable of relation only because they belong together in a more comprehensive thing of the same sort. Streets in a town are related because they belong to, and help make up, a town with a certain overall shape.

Bradley contends that this is true of every case where things are related. This is always a matter of the way in which they go together to make up a more comprehensive thing. He also argued that the more comprehensive thing was in some way more real than what it included, in the sense that any conception of the *parts*, or better *aspects*, which left out how they figured in the whole led to a distortion of our conception of them. A different example may help to bring out what he had in mind. There is a school of psychiatrists which holds that there are not so much disturbed individuals, as disturbed families. If one tries to form a conception of a supposedly disturbed person on the basis of what one can learn about him on his own, one's conception of him will not merely be incomplete, it will be actually wrong. If that is so it is an instance of a principle which Bradley thought universal, that parts or aspects are misconceived when studied in detachment from the wholes to which they belong, a thesis captured in the slogan that wholes are more real than their parts. It is not denied, of course, that in practice we must rely on conceptions of individual things which ignore their participation in certain larger wholes.

It follows from this that the whole universe is more real than any of its parts or aspects. Obviously we cannot grasp the complete character of the universe as a whole, but that means that there is some element of misconception in the way in which we understand every individual thing in the world.

As to the reasons for holding that wholes are, in this sense, more real than their parts, it would take us too far afield to examine them. An impression of the basis of the thesis may be gained by considering how the face of an angel, say, figuring in a certain painting, but first seen alone (in reproduction or by covering up of the remainder) alters the character it has even within its very own bounds when seen as making its own particular contribution to just that whole. You may say that the physical pigments do not alter. But then, for an idealist like Bradley, for whom experience is the only true reality, it suffices to show that every experience owes its character to the context of other experiences within which it occurs, and that no experience had at one moment has a character intelligible (whether to others or to the person himself) apart from knowledge of past influences which have brought it about.

If all this is so, centres of experience can only stand in relation to each other, belong in the same universe, and indeed only thus stand to their own past, if all centres of experience, past, present and future, are aspects of a whole, homogeneous in character with themselves, and more real than them. This, the absolute idealist argues, can only be some vast cosmic consciousness, a kind of infinite centre of experience, of which all other, and in contrast to it finite, centres of experience figure as elements helping to make up the quality and pattern of its total way of feeling its own being. This infinite totality of experience is usually called the Absolute.

Just as a finite centre of experience at any particular moment is not composed of distinct sensations, images, feelings, etc. somehow glued together to make it up, but is a unitary whole within which these exist as inseparable aspects, coloured through and through by everything else going on within the total experience, so is each of them really a kind of throb of feeling, or perhaps a counter it uses in its own eternal grasp of its own nature, within the one infinite absolute experience. That absolute experience includes within its being all centres of experience which, from my point of view thinking now, lie in the past and future, as well as present ones. The idea that the past simply vanishes into nothingness, taken seriously, would mean that there was no such thing as historical truth, or even historical error, since there would be nothing which the historian could even be wrong about. But if the past does not vanish into nothingness, it must be something which is from an ultimate point of view eternally present, and that means the future must be eternally present too, since as the future of this present time it is no different in status from this very present the past of which is really composed of nows. Each centre of experience, considered as something of a moment, has the illusion that it is passing away into nothingness, but this is an illusion which the Absolute gives to itself, in experiencing itself through the medium of these distinct centres, and frees itself from in that total experience of everything which it also enjoys.

We may modify, then, the provisional statement that what experiences the individual centre of experience is simply itself. There is some truth in this, but it is truer still to say that the universe as a whole, that is, the Absolute, feels itself within each centre, and as feeling itself therein gives itself the illusion that it is a separate being from itself feeling itself in another centre, an illusion, of course, corrected for it in its own total experience, and one which we, or it in us, can see through in moments of illumination. Bradley admits that we cannot conceive precisely how all this is possible. It cannot be quite like the unity of our own finite experience, for the different elements in that do not have any sense of themselves as separately experiencing individuals, for if they did, we would participate with them in that sense. Still, Bradley thinks we can attain a partial intuitive idea of this as being the way things are and can see, intellectually, that it must be so.

Absolute idealists have differed as to whether their conception of the

Absolute is to be taken as a philosophically improved conception of God. Bradley himself was among those who thought it misleading to call it 'God', but followers of his have disagreed. Although Bradley seems to have had only a slight interest in Eastern religions, indeed he was of his generation in having a firm commitment to the superiority of Western culture, his view surely has some affinity to the conceptions of the divine found in Vedanta Hinduism. Certainly Bradley was of an essentially religious disposition, but he was mostly unsympathetic to the organized Christianity of his day and intimated that he thought a new religion might be needed, and might come. He urged, however, that one should not necessarily identify the truest philosophy with the best religion, since the latter being a practice rather than a theory may even flourish best on ideas which the philosopher cannot accept as literal truth. On all these matters, he was admirably open-minded and unpretentious, regarding the philosophy he advocated as valuable for its demonstration of the falsity of materialistic conceptions of the world and in its opening people's minds to spiritual dimensions of reality. This open-mindedness extended to such matters as a life after death. Certainly the individual life has some significance in the eternal scheme of things, but that might or might not mean that it had an individual destiny beyond the grave. Our personal task is to express in our lives, in ways suited to our particular situations, those eternal values which we know are somehow sustained at the heart of being by the Absolute.

But how do we know that the Absolute is in any sense good? Actually Bradley denied that it was, in any proper meaning of the term, in which it stands for a contrast which holds only within the human sphere. Yet he did call the Absolute perfect. Essentially his line of thought is that all defects in individuals come from their finitude and conflicts with each other, from which arise such evils as malice, despair and so forth. The Absolute cannot be frustrated, since there is nothing beyond itself, it cannot strive, because it experiences itself in an eternal now, which includes the strains of temporal existence within it, as we may hear a melody in one single act of apprehension, but which cannot as a whole be straining after anything and must therefore be content with itself, and therefore find nothing within itself not satisfactory when seen in context.

It cannot be said that Bradley's own treatment of the place of evil in the universe is very satisfactory. A much better attempt to grapple with the problem is found in the philosophy of another absolute idealist, the American Josiah Royce (1855–1916), who sought to show how all the highest goods we know contain evil as an essential ingredient, and that

71

therefore the universe would lose the highest goods did it lack evil. It seems to me, however, that the absolute idealist need not try to show that evil is somehow good, or even something which ministers to the good. It is enough if he can satisfy us that great evil may be a necessity in any universe, and that therefore the Absolute can delight in its own being provided only the good in the universe is such that it is worth, though not improved by, the evil, which, as such, remains detestable.

A usual solution to the problem of evil in a theistic context which appeals to human freedom is not available to the absolute idealist. It is not that he will be a physical determinist, of course, but he does think that every detail of the universe is so impregnated by its relation to everything else that it could not have been otherwise in its context. In some way it is necessary that I act just as I do. That does not mean that it does not spring from my personal choice, or could have been predicted apart from knowledge of my unique personality, and it is arguable that if it does so spring in a manner unique to me, it is a free act in any sense of real significance. But free or not, it is built into reality eternally that that is how I act. We shall be taking up these themes in our chapter on Spinozism. (My own personal view of existence, I may as well say here, is a synthesis of Bradleyism and Spinozism.)

Whether we think the Absolute can reasonably be called 'God' or not, Bradley is surely right that it is not a person. It has no environment and it does not act in time. If it is in any sense personal, that is because the relations of persons existing within it are an especially significant aspect of its being. One may even suggest that *all* persons are in it, and aspects of it, in a sense perhaps not altogether different from that in which the persons of the Trinity are present in the God of Christian orthodoxy.

What most marks it off from the Christian God is that it did not create, but is, the universe. By the Absolute we mean the totality of all that is existing as a self-experiencing unity. Some personalization of it in religious experience may be appropriate, but that is not the truth about it.

The most effective argument against the Bradleyan position was urged by William James, who said that individual centres of experience can somehow penetrate each other, and thereby even constitute a sort of whole together, without all belonging together in one whole. Even if I have to be together in a whole with other persons to stand in relation to them, may it not be that I stand in relation to one person by belonging to the same family, and to another by belonging to the same firm? Doubtless these are not quite the sort of wholes we must postulate if we are to grasp how centres of experience belong together and communicate, but the essential point seems promising. Bradley would answer, however, that if the family and firm are to be in relation to each other they must belong in some greater unity together, and this means that ultimately all centres must come together in the Absolute.

But where has the physical world gone in this scheme of things? Bradley answers that the object side of a centre of experience, when we take ourselves to be confronted with some material reality, is, hallucination apart, not a mere appearance of the physical, but is the physical itself in the only proper sense. Thus there are partial physical worlds existing in many different centres. Fortunately for human and animal communication, these partial physical worlds dovetail into each other in such a way that they lend themselves to being conceived as parts of one vast physical world transcending what is found in any one centre. In thus conceiving them we have to postulate physical realities which fill out what is given in experience, but which, so far as we know, have no actual existence in any centre. For reasons we have adumbrated, the idea that there really is such a physical reality is ultimately incoherent. However, it is not so incoherent that it cannot be used, and indeed must be, as a way of thinking, through which we learn what we have to do in order to bring various physical realities into existence as actual objects of perception within a centre. As a useful idea, both in general and in the details which constitute geography and science, it even has a perfectly respectable kind of human truth, and only has to be rejected when we seek a fundamental insight into being.

Bradley, in this connection, develops the interesting idea that there may be communities of conscious beings inhabiting quite different such physical worlds from ours. The object aspects of their centres would dovetail into each other so that they construct the conception of a total physical world common to them all, but there would be no direction within their world which leads or points to ours. That does not rule out the possibility of influence of beings in one world on those of another, or of their worlds upon each other, nor that an individual with a sense of personal continuity might 'wake up' to find himself in another world. The experiences of a Swedenborg might be a case of this, and perhaps some spiritualistic phenomena. Bradley was open-minded on these matters too, though he deplored the idea that they bore on anything of real spiritual significance. True spiritual values are, in principle, as realizable, or as difficult to realize, in any one such world as in any other.

But what explains the fact that those personal object worlds, which we do not dismiss as dreams, dovetail into each other and have sufficient individual orderliness to sustain, and be usefully operable on upon the basis of, the imaginative construction of a common physical world? The answer must lie in the unified nature of the absolute experience of which we are all aspects, and in the way in which the whole of things somehow expresses itself partially in each of its constituents. That is only the vaguest of answers, but our ignorance does not trouble Bradley, for it does not cast doubt upon that general scheme of things he believes himself to have established as certain truth by arguments which, in my opinion, are very strong.

One possibility, already touched on, is that we belong within a system of centres of experience much vaster than that which consists of the experiences of men and animals, and that what gives us a common physical world is the action upon us of centres of experience of some lowlier kind. These would then function for us somewhat as the things in themselves of Kant, though Bradley strongly disliked that expression, for at least we know that these lower centres, if they exist, do so by feeling their own being and dimly sensing their interaction with other centres. Bradley thought this no more than a possibility, certainly not required by his general theory. These centres would be, like us, an aspect of the Absolute's own fullness of experience, which, in any case, far transcends anything of which we can know. To me it seems that this 'panpsychist' doctrine rounds out the absolute idealist theory in a manner essential if it is to do justice to the undeniable thereness of nature.

The idealisms of Berkeley and Kant were used as, though certainly not merely concocted in the service of, a defence of a fairly conventional kind of Christian belief against materialism. This is true despite the profoundness of Kant as a moral philosopher. But to what general vision of the good life does absolute idealism point?

It shares one important feature with Berkeleyism, namely that it sets out to rescue us from the feeling that when we commune with nature in solitude we are mere dupes. Both philosophers have a strong sense of that impoverishment of nature which arises when we think that in its true being it answers only to the descriptions given of it in physics. Both materialists and dualists rob nature of all its colour and beauty, the first by eliminating them altogether from the scheme of things, the second by treating them as mere subjective effects in the mind. The idealist, for whom the real physical world is that which we immediately encounter in our own experience, and which really possesses every quality manifestly present there, leaves it its evident glories while holding that what lies 'behind' it are not colourless particles in pointless movement but either God's own enjoyment of his imagery or some fuller experience within the Absolute. If the panpsychist version of absolute idealism is adopted we may surmise that the special appeal of certain places is that they stimulate a breaking down of those barriers that give us a false sense of separation from the whole of things, and bring us into refreshing contact with the so-called lower grades of sentience.

Thus we have the paradox, as it seems at first, that the philosophy which is usually thought of as denying the reality of the physical actually attaches a higher value to our enjoyment of it than do dualism or materialism. In the case of Bradleyan idealism this extends to the significance for us of our own bodily being. We saw that the Cartesian postulates the possibility of a form of existence in which we have no sensory experience, and tends to look on this as a hoped-for liberation from slavery to the body, while the materialist uses his best logical devices to explain away sensory experience altogether. For a Bradleyan, the idea of a mind with no sensory experience is an absurdity. One of his main objections to materialism is that it asks us to think of physical reality as a kind of abstract structure with no sensible or aesthetic quality, and he would think that the same kind of false abstraction was at work in the Cartesian attempt to think of a thought devoid of all sensible subject matter and symbols. So he will hardly decry the value of sense experience in the fullest sense.

If one considers that physical mysticism of D. H. Lawrence for which the intellect which seeks to detach itself from its bodily being is weakening its connection with those depths from which comes all true fulfilment, one finds an attitude which coheres well with Bradleyism, as does the conception of deep sexual experience as the core of significance in human existence. Bradley is mostly the reticent Victorian about these things, but there are references to 'carnal passion' which suggest that he would have sympathized with Lawrence to an extent which would surprise those who think of idealism as a wishy-washy attempt to cleanse one's spiritual hands of the physical. Certainly the sympathy would have been limited, but it is worth dwelling on the fact that there is nothing in such idealism pointing to disdain of the body. After all, when one is engaged in bodily activity, the self side of experience largely coincides with one's body as it exists there, as that with which the centre as a whole especially identifies itself.

The main message of absolute idealism, however, is that we are each aspects of a larger whole which has its own larger life, and that if we follow the leadings which come as from the deeper levels of our being, which are dimly continuous with the whole to which we belong, we will gain the sense that our strivings to fulfil our own potentialities play a part in some deep, if largely hidden, significance possessed by the universe as a whole. Those leadings are more particularly to be trusted which bring us into union with our fellows, human and perhaps even animal. Our separation from these is an illusion, and though this separateness has its role in the scheme of things, as allowing the Absolute to express itself in differentiated ways which increase the value of the universe, it is, all the same, an illusion, and we are nearer to the core of things when we partly transcend it in cooperative ethical, cultural and intellectual endeavours and in mutual aid.

FOUR

MAN AND WORLD AS WILL: THE VISION OF SCHOPENHAUER

I now turn to a very different type of theory of existence from those we have so far considered – to the theories of existence of Schopenhauer and, in the next chapter, Nietzsche. These are far more anguished theories of existence than any we have so far encountered, and speak to our emotions in a much more personal way. Each theory, however, is rooted in wonderings, speculations and arguments closely related to those we have so far considered, particularly in our chapter on idealism.

Schopenhauer's starting point lies in acceptance of the key contentions of idealism, particularly in the version of idealism developed by Immanuel Kant. We have seen that for Kant the physical world, the world of things in space and time, only exists as object of the human mind's awareness. It is the way something which is not physical at all, which lacks the essential traits of what mark something as physical, appears to us. What the things in themselves, or the thing in itself, are or is, which presents itself to us under this guise, we have no way of knowing. Our knowledge is of a world which is definitely there for us, and we must be content with this.

Actually Kant thought our moral consciousness, and intimations provided by religious faith, gave us ground to hope that the reality behind the merely apparent world of physical things is one which somehow makes sense of morality and religion in a way which merely physical nature does not, but how it makes sense of them must remain unknown to us, at least in this life. We do not even know what we ourselves really are. Descartes was wrong in thinking that one knows the very essence of one's own mind. One only knows one's very own mind and self as it appears to itself, and not as it really is.

We are not, however, concerned here with Kant's theory except in so far as large parts of it were taken over by Schopenhauer, and it will be best to turn to these ideas as they develop and change in the hands of the latter, a thinker of a very different stamp, with a much more dramatic picture of the world.

Schopenhauer (1788–1860) thought that Berkeley and Kant had established that the physical world only exists as object experienced by conscious subjects such as ourselves. (He rightly regards Kant's position as essentially a more sophisticated version of Berkeleyism, despite Kant's having denied this.) A physical reality is something spread out in space, lasting through time, and interacting with other things according to eventually ascertainable physical laws. For a whole host of reasons we cannot think that anything of this sort is really in existence except as something which is given in some mind's perceptual experience. Try to imagine something like a house as it is in itself, and not as it reveals itself in the perceptions one has of it from outside and inside, and in one's awareness of the protection it gives one from the elements, and you imagine a mere blank. Imagining a physical thing is always imagining it as it exists for some conscious subject, and we can make no sense of it existing otherwise. Or rather, when we speak, as of course we do, of physical things existing unperceived by anyone, we can only mean that they are available for perception, and as objects one can make use of in perceptually guided manipulation. The characteristics we speak of them as possessing in the absence of perceivers are what we have learnt we can perceive if we take appropriate steps. Neither they nor their characteristics are there in any other sense, considered as objects existing in space and time. The same goes for space and time themselves.

Schopenhauer's treatment of these matters is much more complex than this, while there are also questions one would expect him to deal with concerning which I find no very clear answer in him. Since this is not an exposition of Schopenhauer's thought in detail, and not the place to discuss how he would have answered certain questions had he been asked for clarification on them, I have already simplified, and also in certain respects rounded out, his position to make it more coherent. In this way I can get to the heart of his message, I believe, more effectively. These remarks apply to a greater or lesser extent to my treatment of all the philosophers considered in this book.

In agreeing with Kant that physical reality, and space and time themselves, have no existence outside human (or perhaps animal) consciousness of them, Schopenhauer also agrees with Kant that there must be some reality in itself which somehow registers itself in our consciousness as the physical world, though not physical in its own true character. Corresponding to each physical thing which we perceive, or might perceive, there must be a thing in itself with which we somehow interact so as to produce perceptual consciousness of just such a physical thing. There must, indeed, be some variety in the realm of things in themselves, or of the thing in itself, which settles whether I see a tree or a house. That whatever I see or perceive is spread out in three dimensions and endures through time is determined, according to both philosophers, by the nature of my consciousness, rather than the particular element in the realm of things in themselves to which I am responding. Space and time somehow reflect my own being, and belong to it, rather than to that to which I am responding.

It is not exactly that the thing in itself which corresponds to the house I live in (or the aspect of the thing in itself, if it should be rather more like one thing than many things, something as doubtful as everything else about the realm of things in themselves or of the thing in itself, a point I have so far marked by clumsy locutions like this, but which henceforth I shall take as understood) causes me to have the perceptual experience I do. Causation really only holds between objects in the perceivable world presented to consciousness, not between consciousness itself and that world. Rather, in some way or other the thing in itself is the very thing which I perceive as a house, spread out in space and lasting through time, only, as it really is, it is not spatial or temporal or in any way physical. Schopenhauer thinks that there must be something of which we somehow register the existence in our perceptual experience, and which is what the perceived thing really is. There is no absolute proof of this, but it would be really a kind of madness to think that nothing existed except human perceptual consciousness, and that this was not a registering of the existence of anything at all beyond itself.

Kant thought we just could not know what the things in themselves are which correspond to the objects which we perceive, and which have no existence in the character we perceive them as possessing except as an aspect of our perceptual experience. But Schopenhauer believes we have a clue to the nature of these things in themselves which can take us quite a long way in understanding the true nature both of the world and of ourselves.

This clue lies in the fact that there is one reality which each of us knows, not simply as it appears, but as it really is in itself. This is our own will. Whereas I know everything else in the world only as an object which can exhibit itself to my perceptual experience (or which is posited to fill out what can thus present itself and is an object of essentially the same sort, with spatial and other characteristics which things can only possess for an onlooker's awareness of them), in the case of my own will I become aware of it, not from some external perspective on it which brings perspectival distortions, but directly from the inside. This is because this will is what essentially I am, and my knowledge of it is the will's own lighting up to itself. So it presents itself as a hypothesis that the internal reality of things in general is something of the same basic sort as my own will.

Moreover, it is not simply the case that the will, that is, his or her own will for each of us, is known immediately in its inherent nature, but that in thus knowing it I also grasp that it is the very same thing, experienced from the inside, which both others and myself know from the outside as the physical activity of an object in space. For when I perform an action, say of obtaining, preparing and consuming food, I recognize this action as a perceivable series of movements of my organism which others can see from the outside, and of which I have my own perceptual and theoretical awareness, an awareness which is of the same essential type as that of an external observer, but I am also aware of it from the inside as a process of willing.

It is not that the process of willing is identified as the cause of my physical actions, but that it comes to me, once I reflect on the matter, as an indubitable fact that the willing and its physical manifestation are the same thing grasped in two different ways – in the latter case as it appears from outside itself, in the former as it is for itself.

There is, then, one bit of the physical world for each of us which he knows in its very essence, as it really is. To some extent at least I know what my own physical organism, when it is engaged in deliberate action, really is, namely *will*. This will is not in itself spatial – rather is it a drive towards certain ends which shifts between states of satisfaction and dissatisfaction. This drive which is experienced from within as my willing presents itself to the onlooker as a series of physical movements of an object in space. That object, and its movements, considered as something running its course in space is part of, and in its most general characteristics (three-dimensionality, weight or mass, for example) akin to, a much vaster world of things in space. This interconnection and homogeneity of character which links all physical things suggests that what they are in themselves must possess an equal homogeneity which can allow them to interact with each other in their real nature in such a way as to produce the visible phenomena of the world. Thus if will or drive is known to be the inner character, the true essence, of one part of the physical world, it seems that the true essence of the rest of the physical world must be something of the same general sort, a fact we can mark by using 'will' (perhaps in a somewhat extended sense, but marking a real identity of character between what we usually so call, and that to which we now extend the term), to refer to the 'in itself' of physical nature as a whole. Of course, having once seen that will is the 'in itself' of our own bodies, to take this as being true also of other human beings and of animals is a matter of mere common sense; the recognition that the inner being of the whole of nature is will is likely to meet with more resistance. However, the case for this conclusion is very strong, and it becomes still stronger, according to Schopenhauer, when we study natural phenomena with this interpretation in mind as a possibility. More and more we will find the recognition unavoidable that what scientists learn of the basic *forces* at work in nature, and of the *laws* of nature that govern them (these really being different ways of looking at the same fact), represents an external grasp upon the different sorts of will or drive which are what the phenomena exhibiting these forces, or falling under these laws, are in their own inner being. For we know they must have an inner being, must be something in themselves, since their physical characteristics are something they only possess for an observer. In suggesting that this inner being is will we are only supposing that an equal homogeneity holds at the level of inner reality as holds in external appearance. Schopenhauer illustrates the fruitfulness of this interpretation by a quite detailed consideration of all the basic forces at work in nature, as recognized by the science of his time. He would have had to alter the details of this treatment if he were writing today, but I do not think that his basic positions suffer by recent scientific developments.

One difficulty in understanding Schopenhauer is as to what exactly it is to which one is to turn one's attention in order to identify that will or willing which he tells us we will recognize as being our actions known from the inside. It is evidently not the feeling of one's limbs in motion, nor feelings of strain and exertion, that are in question. Nor is it any image one may have of the goal one is pursuing, or verbal descriptions one gives oneself of this goal. All these, for Schopenhauer, are ways of perceiving or thinking about the object world, the world in space and time. The will, as he understands it, seems to be some more deep-seated thrusting forward which he thinks one senses at the basis of such phenomena, but it is at the least less obvious than Schopenauer thought it that, if you remove all such feelings, images and descriptions, there is anything left to will as one experiences it.

Actually Schopenhauer seems to have taken rather different positions on these questions at different stages in the development of his thought In his earlier writings 'will' seems to stand in a fairly straightforward way for the itchings of desire, the restlessness which lies behind much activity, and for pleasure and pain in the satisfaction and dissatisfaction of desire, or at least for something of which these are states which reveal it in a fairly direct fashion. Later he came to think of will itself as not known quite as it is in itself, so that our experiences of willing, as we would call them, only bring us nearer to insight into that which we are as things in ourselves than does perceptual experience inform us of the real essence of what we perceive, without giving us any really genuine insight into its being. This seems rather to rob of its force the whole thesis that we know ourselves as essentially will, since 'will' virtually becomes a mere name for the thing in itself, whatever it is. For that reason I prefer the earlier formulations, and shall abide by them, though certainly some of Schopenhauer's views do demand the later and more mysterious conception. The difference is anyway one of degree. He always holds that the very act of self-observation produces an artificial division between observing subject and observed will which destroys the true character of will.

Since I have a great respect for the theory of Schopenhauer, and think he was on to something really important, I shall develop it along lines which I think make the best sense of it. So perhaps we may take it that by will is meant a kind of feeling of yearning, or longing, or restless itching to be rid of one's present state and situation and into another, and that Schopenhauer thinks we can detect this feeling as a perpetual dim background to perceptual experience which is more constant and essential to our being than any particular goal we set ourselves. Our particular goals get attached to this constant yearning and then it steers action towards them, but as soon as that goal is achieved the yearning will attach itself to another goal, since it is the will or yearning which makes us look for something to direct our action towards rather than the thought of the goals which brings the yearning into existence. It seems, however, that yearning of various different types exists in the world, and that the different qualities of yearning associate themselves with different sorts of goals. It is these different qualities of yearning which make the difference between the character of one person and another and ultimately between the different forces at work in nature in general.

Thus in its inner nature all physical reality consists of innumerable different feelings of yearning which somehow impinge on each other and struggle against each other. Associated with at least some of these feelings of yearning, those which are what constitute the distinctive aspect of the 'in itself' of humans and animals, are images or representations of a world spread out in space, and altering over time, which give that particular node of yearning a sense of itself as an individual physical object among others, but which are really the registering in an ultimately delusive medium or code of the relations of conflict and rapprochement between it and other nodes of yearning. Actually I find it very difficult to see how there could be any such nodes of yearning which did not have some such representations associated with them to guide their interaction with others, but Schopenhauer would seem to deny this. Where the yearnings are not associated with any representations which steer them towards the production of certain effects on themselves and on other nodes of yearning, and they interact with other things in complete blindness to their situation, they are designated as unconscious by Schopenhauer. It is unclear whether this precludes these yearnings from being in any sense genuine feelings. If it does I personally can see no sense to calling them instances of will or yearning, for unless they somehow feel their own existence they seem too unlike anything we encounter in ourselves under such headings as 'will' or 'desire' to be thus labelled. Although Schopenhauer is not very explicit on the matter I incline to think he did suppose that they are to be thought of as some kind of low-level feelings of yearning in some proper sense of feeling.

If the inner being of my body is my will, it might seem that when I cease to exist as an individual will my body will cease to exist. What then is a corpse? The answer is that my body when I am alive and awake and acting is the presentation to perception (whether my perception or someone else's) of a whole complex of different levels of will. My distinctively human and personal behaviour is the appearance of that personal will which reveals itself to some extent to self-observation, as we have seen, as intertwined with lower, less articulate forms of willing which manifest themselves in all those aspects of my body which can be adequately treated by such sciences as chemistry and physics. When I die, perhaps also when I am in deep sleep, that higher level of will lapses, but my body is still there to be perceived as the registering in the perceiver's consciousness (the perceiver himself being a node of will with a guiding system of images or representations associated with it) that there is a particular pattern of yearnings present of the type which correspond to phenomena adequately treated by physics and chemistry.

What is it that all these feelings of yearning are yearning for? Schopenhauer says that the will is the will to live or exist. Thus what they will or yearn for is their own existence. Since they do exist, it would seem then that they have got what they want. Perhaps then we should say that it is continuation of their existence or survival that they will, and that the effects they produce are all, more or less consciously, directed to this end. But surely the dissatisfaction which is of their essence is something they wish to shake off, and since they could not shake it off without ceasing to be (since they are nothing but such dissatisfied yearning) there is a sense in which they yearn to cease? Now it would fit in rather well with much of Schopenhauer's outlook to see the will as something which is paradoxically both a will to continue and to cease, but he does not develop a paradox along these lines. The view it suggests of human reality, and ultimately of all reality, as 'a useless passion' (to use an expression Sartre applies to human being for reasons somewhat of this sort) is certainly Schopenhauerian in spirit, but we come closer to what Schopenhauer seems actually to have held if we take it that his expression 'will to live' (where 'live' covers the existence willed for itself by what we would ordinarily call the inanimate, as well as existence as a living being in the ordinary sense) is inadequate to express the vision of things he is really getting at.

What his view comes to rather is that will or yearning is a will to survive at all costs, but also a will to find some kind of quietus in which its restlessness will be assuaged. It is the will for its perpetual continuation but in a form in which it does not have to struggle for ever more. As such the will is directed at an impossible end. Its very essence or being is this constant yearning, so that it could not possibly find rest and peace without ceasing to be. This is very close to the idea just touched on that the will is at once a will to be and to cease, but though this is a turn which Schopenhauer's thought took when it became the inspiration of Wagner in the motivations of both Tristan and Isolde (Wagner was an explicit Schopenhauerian), we cannot ascribe it as such to Schopenhauer himself, seeing that for him the will's denying of itself is a quite special turn it takes in saints (as we shall be seeing shortly), but no part of its normal being. So I think we must say that for him the will is directed at its own survival, but preferably in a form which is unfortunately incompatible with its very essence. It wants to be a satisfied will, but this is a contradiction in terms.

Schopenhauer recognizes, of course, that on the face of it different wills are directed at different ends. All human beings and animals want nourishment, sexual satisfaction and release from pain of various kinds, but only some men want to learn mathematics, and even in the realm of the basic desires just mentioned the food and the sexual gratification sought differs greatly from person to person. His view seems to be that these divergences are of two sorts. First, our basic characters lay down in general terms the kinds of gratification we want, and every man's basic character is different from every other's (though they are variations on a common human theme). Outside humanity basic character is the same for all members of an animal species, and, at the inanimate level, the same for all physical phenomena subject to the same laws of nature. But secondly, in the case of human beings (and perhaps of animals), there is acquired character which consists in one's desire to achieve all sorts of further goals by means of certain characteristic types because one has learnt that these goals are themselves means to the goals set by one's basic character. Thus a taste for the gratifications provided by mathematical calculation could in principle either be built into one's basic character, or one might have learnt the utility of skill in such calculation for satisfying some other more basic need. The different ways in which different human beings behave, and in which different species of animals behave, and the different sorts of effect we trace to different basic forces and laws of nature, are all a matter of the different sorts of gratification to which the different sorts of longing or will which are the basic reality of the world are attuned or have become addicted. That seems to be roughly what Schopenhauer's view on this matter comes to, though put somewhat differently. So although he sometimes writes as though all will had just one and the same goal, mere survival, it seems that he meant survival in some particular state of gratification. What is, however, common to all willing, if Schopenhauer is right, is that it can never reach satisfaction, since though it can have shifts between somewhat more pleasing and less pleasing states, the only thing which is there to be satisfied or otherwise is will and will can only be there in the form of an itching to be on to something else. Apart from this and related arguments of an *a priori* kind (arguments based on supposed insights into the very essence of things), Schopenhauer amasses all sorts of more concrete evidence about the misery of all existence. All experience, as well as the very nature of the case, shows that there are only two states in which a human being can exist for any time; either wretchedness from some kind of deprivation, or boredom from the lack of any need which prompts to action. (I set aside for the moment a third possible state of freedom from bondage to the will which may be possible for saints.) Schopenhauer was the first great pessimistic philosopher in the Western tradition. Western philosophy till then, Schopenhauer contended with some justice, had always attempted to provide an at least momentary comfort by disguising the true horrors of human existence (into many unpleasant details of which Schopenhauer goes at length and a sufficiency of which any reader can doubtless recall for himself).

I have spoken of different wills willing different things. It is now time to turn to an aspect of Schopenhauer's thought so far passed over, namely his view that strictly there are not many wills, not many individualized nodes of yearning, but that all the yearnings in the world are somehow but aspects of one vast cosmic yearning which is what the physical universe as a whole is in itself. This vast cosmic yearning to exist and be gratified certainly in some manner individuates itself into such particular nodes of yearning as you and I, dogs, cats, spiders, the gravity which tugs the earth towards the sun and the inertia which keeps the earth thrusting forward in its original line of movement, but Schopenhauer speaks of these as different grades or types of objectification of *the Will*, urging that ultimately there is but one will, one cosmic yearning, whose wretchedness includes the sense that it consists in a multiplicity of different yearnings normally at war with one another and surviving only by preying on one another. The yearning which is the core of me and that which is the core of you are really one single yearning which is in a state of estrangement from itself.

Schopenhauer's main official reason for urging this is that counting only makes sense where the counted objects are distinguished by their spatial or temporal position. Where there is no such separation of objects one from another there can be no definite number of them. But will, considered as thing in itself, is not in space or time. It is only its appearances to perception which are thus separated, and if you say that the perceptual experiences and the wills to which they belong are many, this is something one can only make sense of if one confuses them with the bodies they animate. I am not myself asking the reader to believe that this is true, but it is Schopenhauer's claim, so far as that can be presented briefly. Thus the many-ness of our different willings or longings is an illusion.

It is an obvious objection that even if number only has application to objects separated in space and time, that does not show that there is but one will, but rather that it makes no sense to talk of one or many here. Schopenhauer meets this objection, which he anticipates, roughly by saying that the oneness of the Will which he asserts is not *one* considered as the first number in a process of counting, but oneness as a lack of real separation, and that in the absence of space and time, the only conceivable forms of separateness of one thing from another, this non-numerical kind of oneness should be asserted. Even if this were granted, I think many people would say that willing goes on in time even if not in space.

Schopenhauer would perhaps say that the dating of acts of will, and the settling of questions as to which of us willed something first, or even of the temporal order of my own acts of will, is only possible, and only intelligible, if we treat acts of will as events in the perceivable physical world, thus not as they really are. There is something in this, but it must be admitted that the whole notion of timeless willing, and the view that our own acts of will are not really temporal at all, is obscure indeed, if not thoroughly incoherent. Actually I do myself think that there is a sense in which time is unreal and that nothing really is in time, as we normally understand the term, but I do not think that the sense in which I would assert this is Schopenhauer's, and in the end I suspect that Schopenhauer's view here does not make sense, though something very like it, which I shall indicate later, does and would have served his turn as well.

Whatever the merits of Schopenhauer's argumentation that our wills are not truly separate, and the vagueness of his particular way of developing the point, the more general aspects of his viewpoint accord here with the reports mystics give of what they believe has been revealed to them, and also with the occasional intuitions of many more ordinary people. So even if we can hardly accept it as proved by him, or very successfully articulated, his vision of the world of rival wills (the background to nature as perceived) as being itself in its turn an illusion which some ultimate act, state or process (the contrasts between these terms do not apply here) of cosmic longing gives itself, living through it in each of us, might still be the faltering adumbration of a truth.

The view that space and time are only a pervasive aspect of the way the world appears to the subject of consciousness (which is not itself truly temporal or spatial, and so not truly plural, so that as subjects of consciousness you and I are one, being simply the universal will taking up various different perspectives on its own being), and not pervasive aspects of reality, that is of the one Will, as it truly is, is tied up in Schopenhauer's philosophy with a doctrine which I am largely ignoring in my exposition, at the cost of oversimplifying, but as I am inclined to think, also improving his theory of existence. This is his view of the various species of animals and plants, and of the main basic forces of inanimate nature, as not really consisting of many different individuals even to the extent that the race of human beings do, but that all members of a given species are a single individual, and therefore one single act of will or longing, which only appears as many to minds which see things as divided in space and time. The identity of the will between all members of a single species is not simply the singleness of the cosmic will. They are not even many for themselves in the sense in which human beings are. There is some sense in which the single will has given itself the illusion of being many human beings (so that each human is like a distinct species), but the illusion that there are many tigers, say, is only an illusion on the part of the human being who watches them, rather than on the part of the Will as it feels itself in the tigers. Or if this is not quite Schopenhauer's view, his actual view is even less intelligible. His theory seems to me to make much better sense, and to follow much more persuasively from his main line of reasoning, if we take it that the illusory self-differentiation of the one cosmic act, state or process of willing is into many willings, each of which constitutes the inner reality of one particular physical organism or thing (rather than a species or type) such as has some power to hold itself together as a persisting entity.

The essential thing is that all the processes of willing which struggle against each other in the world and which, so far as they have any kind of developed consciousness, are aware of each other as different objects distributed in space and interacting in a common time, are in some sense or other really one. This makes it even more tragic that, in their desperate craving to carry on existing (one speaks of them as having this craving, but in fact they just *are* this craving), with the gratifications suited to their particular quality, they normally only see each other as hostile enemies. And indeed this is what they are, since their individual existence such as it is, and their private gratifications, can only be won at the cost of each other. As this situation presents itself under the guise of objects existing in space and time they either are each other's food, or they are rivals for food. Even when not fighting for food, they fight out of sheer hatred. The other main drive which belongs to Will, when it takes the form of animals, namely sexual desire, may (if we think of mammals and birds, say, rather than spiders) seem to show the Will seeking to come to that oneness with another which is, in truth, its real condition. However, Schopenhauer sees sex as ultimately just another way in which we are all enslaved to a craving which is our very selves and which ultimately has no point except to keep the wretched state of craving in existence through descendants who will take on the burden of life, and prevent us, who are really one with our descendants, finding the peace we delude ourselves we find in death. (Not that one will escape this by childlessness, for one is ultimately identical with all creation.) Certainly he would have had no difficulty, in exploring the role of sex in human life, in illustrating various forms of human wretchedness and mutual hatred and exploit- ation thereby; however, as it actually stands, his account of sex is, for once, not primarily directed at showing the wretchedness of life, nor yet at celebrating it as a redeeming joy, but at exhibiting it as the supreme case of the powerlessness of the rational individual, who here is taken over by a power whose aim is preservation of the species.

We may or may not agree that human life, and life in general, is quite as wretched an affair as Schopenhauer sets out to show that it *must be* from its very nature, and that it *is*, by a wealth of illustrations which the interested reader must seek in Schopenhauer's own writings. Schopen- hauer's work made it a fashionable philosophical topic for many decades to weigh up the joys and horrors of human and animal life at large. Granted, however, that his conclusion is that it is as wretched as could be (this is the worst of all possible worlds, he says, since if it was one stage worse it would cease to be, a remark which may set us reflecting on the nuclear holocaust), does his philosophy offer any suggestion as to what, either individually or collectively, we may do about it?

Schopenhauer does think there are certain alleviations, and ultimately a final remedy. He does not think, however, that individuals will find these because they become intellectually convinced of his philosophy, but only if it is in any case in their nature to do so. However, despite this disclaimer, we may, I think, take it that this part of his philosophy offers a kind of recommendation as to what we should do about it all.

First, we may find a certain release in simply realizing that this is how things are. Granted we are to suffer, we will suffer a little less if we have once grasped that there is no real satisfaction to be found in existence.

Second, art and, more generally, the contemplation of the beautiful, offer a kind of respite from the wretchedness of our state. The species of craving which constitutes the 'in itself' of the distinctive aspects of human existence is the most intense and wretched there is, but it has brought along with it the system of images by which our especially highly de- veloped form of will guides itself in its struggle to survive and gratify itself. If we simply contemplate these images for what they are, and also for a kind of intuitive sense they give us of the ultimate nature of the world, and do not utilize them in their original role as means, we can achieve a momentary release from willing. Will has, so to speak, secreted within its own being something which is not will, and it can momentarily escape from itself in contemplating this secretion. Such contemplation is not a gratification of the will, not a pleasure (like food and sex, for example), but a state in which the will as it were momentarily casts off its own very nature. Works of art record such moments of will-less contemplation on the artist's part, and provide an opportunity for such contemplation to the rest of us.

But of course will cannot continue to be itself, to survive, in such a state which is the negation of its own being, so art is a momentary release, rather than a solution. We come somewhat nearer to this in ethical feeling and conduct, which Schopenhauer identifies with sympathy for and empathy with others in their sufferings and the action to which such feeling inspires. In so far as one is a moral being one sees through the illusion of separate identity and takes the other's suffering as what it really is, the suffering of the same single cosmic reality as oneself. Not that one needs to have expressed it to oneself in such language, but that is the insight which one implicitly has. This gives us a kind of release from the self-involvement which is the source of so much of our misery, and may also lead to an alleviation of the sufferings of the others.

The relief which moral feeling and action bring for either the agent or the person or animal one helps is, however, strictly limited. No conscious subject can have an existence which is other than predominantly wretched. For this reason social reforms are of very limited value in solving the human problem. The best one can hope for is unity under a strong government of a not too malevolent kind which will keep people from each other's throats, and prevent the worst ways in which humans abuse each other and animals. Schopenhauer, we may note, praised the English for their concern for the welfare of animals and for the founding of the R.S.P.C.A. (If he knew what the English, and the British generally, allow to go on in their laboratories and farms today, he might have retracted this.)

So moral conduct is primarily of value in somewhat lessening the nastiness of life in particular situations as they arise. Moral concern which leads to efforts to found a society in which human life can be a positive joy for people at large rather than a burden just fosters an illusion which will make the disappointingness of what is provided by so-called social progress harder to bear than it would be otherwise.

The only final solution comes when people become so aware of the futility of life, of the misery of existing as that which they really are, delusively individualized throbs of craving, that they lose all wish to be and to be gratified. This is what happens in the case of the genuine saint, who is always an ascetic who has no concern with living and prospering.

In him the will to live has, as Schopenhauer puts it, denied itself. Or rather, there is only a faint twinkling of it left, hardly enough to sustain the picture of a world of things in space and time, and when he dies this twinkling will utterly cease, and with it the world of which he was conscious, since this consisted in nothing but his picture of it and his will. The will cannot continue to be when it no longer desires, since its desire is its very self, and the world cannot be when the will ceases, since the world is only a delusive picture of the being of the will.

The nature of this solution has puzzled many of Schopenhauer's readers. Presumably when the ascetic saint dies, something ceases to be which does not cease to be when the rest of us die. For otherwise it is not clear what is so special about his cessation. Moreover, it would be a cessation we all could obtain for ourselves, in advance of its inevitable arrival, by suicide. Suicide was condemned by Schopenhauer, however. He contended, rather convincingly, that it is really a supreme assertion of will, the refusing to put up with things if they are not as one wants, and therefore the height of concern with oneself, rather than a denial of the will to be and to be gratified. But above all, there is an illusion if one thinks that it brings the will to an end. That craving which is one's essential self will force its way into existence again for further suffering.

If Schopenhauer believed in personal survival of death, his position would be clear enough. Only he who has denied his very being will avoid survival or reincarnation. But Schopenhauer seems to deny survival of the individual, whether in the manner of reincarnation in this world or in any other form. What survives, he seems to say, is simply the general Cosmic Will, which is what all of us really are. But if this is so, then it would seem that either we must suppose that when the ascetic saint dies and ceases to be more utterly than does the deceased sinner, then the whole Cosmic Will ceases to be, and the world with it, or that he only ceases in that individual way in which the rest of us also do at death. The first alternative seems ruled out by the fact that the world is still here, and yet there have been, as Schopenhauer believes, saints who have died, and the second alternative gives no special point to the death of the ascetic saint.

Schopenhauer does, I think, offer an answer to these problems, but it is expressed somewhat darkly, and is often missed by commentators.

When Schopenhauer denies that there is personal survival he means that after one's death there is no individual, and never will be, who will recall one's experiences and regard them as his own. Moreover, there will not even be an individual whose fate owes anything to the crises one has lived through in this life. There is nothing like Karma, as a kind of impersonal thread of continuity such as Buddhism posits in reconciling its denial of an enduring ego with the meaningfulness of a search for release from the cycle of repeated births. What there is, however (as we have already seen), is a particular quality of will or longing which marks one off from all other persons (except those who will be its next vehicles). This special quality of will, desire, or craving, with its attunement to particular sorts of gratification, is a particular aspect of the one Cosmic Will which will go on and on appearing in different human beings, or some similar organism on another planet perhaps, until it denies itself in one of these vehicles.

When such denial occurs, then, there is a certain whittling away of the Cosmic Will. That cosmic will or craving will finally cease to individualize itself in anything like humans when all the different such qualities of yearning have denied themselves in one of their vehicles.

This at least is what I think Schopenhauer is getting at, when he implies that though there is no reincarnation there is such a thing as what he calls palingenesis. But even so, considerable unclarities remain. To some extent I think Schopenhauer thought these matters beyond our knowledge (beyond all knowledge, indeed, since he recognized no higher knower or knowers). I get the impression, however, that he thought that if all human-type willing, which is willing at its climax of self-consciousness, should whittle itself away in this manner, then the total cosmic will would turn to nothing. For in some manner the human will, as *the Will*'s climax, is the way in which the Will learns that it is something which had much better not be, and when it has learnt this lesson through and through by way of humanity there will be a final end of it.

Of course, the cessation of man in a nuclear holocaust will no more effect this than will an individual suicide. That will not eliminate the peculiarly human level of craving, and the world will remain for it to evolve itself in as a similar species one day in the future. Or at least this is what I think Schopenhauer would say, if he knew of our present situation, and had finally accepted the theory of evolution towards which he seems to have given a favourable nod as an old man.

There is a final twist to Schopenhauer's theory of existence, of great interest which, like the doctrine of palingenesis, is often missed.

When the will denies itself it becomes nothing. Schopenhauer says that his philosophy does not evade the nothingness which is the goal of salvation 'like the Indians, through myths and meaningless words, such as reabsorption in Brahma or the Nirvana of the Buddhists' – it is just *nothing*.

Yet in the end Schopenhauer's evidently quite settled view is a little different from what these words might suggest. For he offers us a remarkable analysis of the conception of 'nothing' which, to boil it down to essentials, comes to this, that by 'nothing' must always be meant 'nothing of that sort', with an interpretation of 'that sort' suited to the occasion. The point is quite simple. 'There is nothing in the cupboard' may mean 'no food' or 'no substantial objects'. It is unlikely to mean 'no atmosphere', and even if it did it would not mean 'no space'. An absolute nothing, so Schopenhauer argues, is meaningless – 'a nothing' is always a relative nothing in the sense indicated.

Thus when we think of the Will as becoming nothing (and are clear that it does not become anything else, if there were anything else, we could identify), we mean, roughly, that it becomes nothing whatever of which we can form any conception. It must still be something, to be a nothing for us, and, from the point of view of that something, it may even be our world and the will which sustains it which is *nothing*.

So Schopenhauer really thinks that when the Will ceases it becomes something so completely inconceivable by us that we delude ourselves in using any other word for it but *nothing* (such as Brahma – more correctly Brahman – or Nirvana if this means more than nothing). It is at any rate not will, and it is not any kind of world of objects or a consciousness confronting such a world. The mystic, however, may have some ineffable sense of what this which we can only call nothing is on its own positive side.

This aspect of Schopenhauer's thought gives more sense to the Will as bringing itself and its world into existence by willing. Perhaps it was this Nothing-for-us which began to crave, and thus became something which was nothing but Will confronting an illusory space–time world.

Since 'time' is somehow part of the illusion, it would seem that the movement of the Nothing into Will and pictured world, and back again after the Will denies itself, must be a transition which takes place out of time. Schopenhauer does not deal with the point, but I think we must take it that what it really amounts to is that there is to Reality in some timeless way a positive assertive craving aspect which gives itself the illusion of a world, and another aspect which, from our point of view, is Nothing, from which the Will and its World is somehow eternally in a state of emergence and return. As to the sense in which time can be unreal, Schopenhauer is more oracular than clear. I can only understand it as meaning that the whole notion of things passing away is a kind of illusion and that every moment of time is eternally there and seems present to itself, however much it is relegated to the past, or thought of as an unknown future, by the consciousness which pertains to other times. That time is, in this sense, unreal can, I believe, be demonstrated – but not here.

One need know little of Vedanta Hinduism and Buddhism to realize that there is much in common between them and Schopenhauer's thought. Schopenhauer was fully aware of this, and delighted in the fact. European knowledge of, and translations from, the scriptures of these religions was only just beginning in Schopenhauer's day – a disciple of Schopenhauer's, Deussen, being pre-eminent in this field. It seems clear, however, that Schopenhauer arrived at his viewpoint from his own personal thought and experience, and building on the quite un-Eastern thought of Kant, before he came to know anything of Eastern religion – a fact which strengthens rather than weakens the case for such an interpretation of the world.

It would be foolish of me to step forward with some attempt at a definitive evaluation of such a grand system as Schopenhauer's. If one is concerned to decide upon its truth, rather than its appeal as a vast intellectual structure simply to be enjoyed as such, I think one should be clear that there is no need either to accept it or reject it as a whole. For myself, I think that things in space and time do have an inner being which is what they really are in themselves, and that this is a kind of felt striving, together with a sense of the other centres of striving with which they are intertwined, a sense which in us takes the form of perception of the physical world. I believe also that there is a fundamental oneness to things, a sense of which inspires moral behaviour. But I do not take very seriously either the possibility or the desirability of the world somehow disappearing because all the striving which is its inner essence comes to deny itself.

[FIVE]

NIETZSCHE AND THE WILL TO POWER

The theories of existence discussed in previous chapters are advanced by their advocates in a highly systematic way. In turning to Nietzsche we are dealing with a thinker who was opposed to systematization, and whose own work conscientiously avoids it, as something which only binds the free-ranging mind in fetters. Yet a fairly definite theory of existence does emerge in his later writings, and it is that which I shall attempt to expound, though at the risk of giving the impression that Nietzsche was more rigidly committed to certain doctrines than he was.

In his earlier writings, especially in *The Birth of Tragedy*, Nietzsche (1844–1900) wrote as a heterodox disciple of Schopenhauer. Throughout his work he makes implicit or explicit comparisons of his positions with Schopenhauer, and it is one legitimate approach to his later positions to see them as representing a derivative from Schopenhauerianism in which a somewhat similar view of how things actually are is made the basis of an utterly different view of how we human beings should respond to their being thus. Both Schopenhauer and Nietzsche agree that will is the very essence of man, and ultimately of the cosmos at large, but while Schopenhauer regards the will as so essentially loathsome that the only salvation there can be is a fundamental alteration in our essence, through which it becomes something quite different, unimaginable by us, Nietzsche sees salvation in a deep acceptance that one is essentially a will seeking to assert itself and a revelling in whatever fullness one can achieve in such self assertion.

Nietzsche agrees with Schopenhauer that if one reflects on one's behaviour, or on that of other men, and if one searches honestly into the depths of one's own being, as revealed in one's private thoughts and feelings, one will find that the essential element present everywhere is will. But whereas Schopenhauer called this will 'will to live', Nietzsche insists that it is much more properly called 'will to power'. That which

95

one is for ever after is not mere survival, but domination and control of whatever there is in the world around one, and indeed of whatever there is within one. One may be so anxious to exert power over things, to make oneself felt in the transformation of how things are which one brings about, that one is much more prepared to die than lose a chance to exercise one's power. Merely to survive in some form or other is far from one's main aim, it is survival as something which is continually extending the sphere of its dominance that one wants.

This will to extend one's own personal domination, the sphere in which one is in control of what goes on, and the degree of that control, can take innumerable different specific forms. All sorts of ordinary personal ambition are examples of it. Joy in fighting, either in individual acts of bellicosity, or by involvement in military conquest, are one main case. Another is artistic creation, which consists above all in the urge to impress one's own personality upon the raw material which one transforms. The scientist's or philosopher's joy in the quest for knowledge is another main type of the will to power. One is delighting in one's power to bring a kind of conceptual order into things which reflects one's own way of thinking.

These forms of will to power are, or may be, honest. We may realize (in whatever terminology) that what we are after in these pursuits is some kind of domination over things. But there are dishonest and corrupt forms of the will to power. People of an essentially weak kind, who are likely to go to the wall and face humiliation in a frankly competitive world, have managed to control strong individuals, by making them ashamed of their strength and their joy in it, and by extorting their pity. When we act out of pity for someone, we have fallen under his sway, and are being dominated by him in a peculiarly subtle way. Persons and groups who set out to evoke pity are utilizing a very potent form of domination which is peculiarly available to the weak, to those, that is, who would be weak without this special power. A less direct way in which the weak may extend their powers is by disseminating a general doctrine of the importance of pity as a civilized value, and also a doctrine according to which exulting in one's own powers is something to be ashamed of. Christianity has been the great agent in Western civilization through which the weak have 'inherited the earth' and robbed the strong of their birthright of exultation in their own strength. I shall come back to this suggestion shortly.

Nietzsche does not offer any metaphysical proof that will to power is the very core of what a human being, and indeed of any other living creature, is. It is rather a hypothesis which is to be accepted because it brings all phenomena, or to the extent that it does, under one general concept in the light of which they are more intelligible, and such that we can get our bearings in deciding how to respond to things more effectively when we have adopted it. Nietzsche is glad to accept the implication of his own theory that the formulation of the hypothesis is an act of Nietzsche's own will to power, and offers a way of exerting power to others who adopt it.

Nietzsche came to believe that it was not only in men and animals that there is will to power at the very core of things, but that this is what all the phenomena of physical nature really are. Ultimately nature consists of innumerable centres of power all seeking to bring surrounding centres under their own influence. Different sorts of centre seek somewhat different sorts of power by somewhat different sorts of means. The laws of nature, as scientists seek to grasp them, really chart in abstract terms the general way in which different sorts of such centre exert their power, and the upshot of their mutual conflict. There is no such thing as a law of nature as some kind of formula which in some strange way holds sway over the elements of nature and forces them to conform to itself. Each centre of power is perpetually expanding its own personal style of domination, and in so far as centres fall into broad general types, this expansion will have the same sorts of effect in comparable circumstances. Nietzsche is inclined to think that science makes the world look much more uniform than it is, and that our classifications bring together as just the same kind of thing, what in fact is only somewhat analogous. However, this kind of forcing of nature into our classifications, and under general laws, satisfies our intellectual will to power, and can serve effectively to promote our practical control over nature, and ability to predict what we will observe under given circumstances, because we only experience things in a rather gross and unrefined way. Our sense experience, and the world as we think of it under the guidance of science, are simply the way in which the activities of other centres of power register themselves inside the centre of power which we are, in such a way that we are guided with some effectiveness in our struggle with them.

All this obviously has much in common with Schopenhauer's vision of things. Nietzsche insists that the notion of the will as a will to live was quite inadequate, but actually the notion of a will to dominate seems to be implicit in Schopenhauer's description of the will to live. There is rather a change of emphasis here than a real change of doctrine. There are other divergences which may be more fundamental.

Nietzsche charges Schopenhauer with thinking of will as some kind of simple invariant quality of experience which one can identify within oneself and surmise as present in others but which has no sort of complexity to it, allowing us to break it down, in our thinking about it, into elements which combine in a certain manner to form it. This, he rightly says, is a travesty of the facts. The state of willing something is a highly complex one, with a variety of discriminable elements, such as a feeling of unease, an idea of something in one's present situation whose removal might stop that unease, thoughts about the means of effecting that removal, muscular feelings of the sort associated with the behaviour required to put these means into practice, and so forth.

All this is quite true. The trouble is that, except when arguing this particular point, one might well think that Nietzsche's will to power is at least almost as at fault as Schopenhauer's will to live in this kind of way. How can one talk so much of will to power as at the very core of every single human being, if will is made up of elements which might presumably exist apart, so that some people would scarcely have wills at all? Even if such falling apart of the elements is not possible, will as a complex phenomenon, capable of taking a variety of forms, is likely to be treated in an over-simplified fashion if we try to subsume all willing as a case of willing for power, or of power seeking to find places in which to vent itself. One can, surely, only make much sense of willing if one grasps the variety of things people will, and the variety of forms their willing takes, and once one has grasped this variety, saying that the object of the will is always *power* is likely to give a quite spurious impression that everyone is really after the same thing.

A more clear-cut difference between the two thinkers is that Nietzsche utterly denies that the plurality of wills is some kind of illusion. The world consists of innumerable centres of will, all battling against each other and striving to dominate each other. For Schopenhauer the world was a scene of endless competitive strife, but in some deep and mysterious way it is the one cosmic will which is struggling against itself. Ethical insight and some degree of detachment from the struggle ensue when the will, feeling itself in one particular apparently distinct consciousness, realizes that the individual it is fighting against is really in the last resort the same cosmic being as itself, in another manifestation. For Nietzsche there is no illusion in the sense we have of our utter distinctness from each other, and anyone who thinks he has any aim other than to promote himself to as dominant a position as possible is deceiving himself and merely being dishonest about what he is really after.

Yet some qualification is required, if we are not to present Nietzsche as thinking of the individual as more fundamental in reality than he actually does. A typical Cartesian dualist (and thinkers of other sorts too) supposes that the sameness of an individual over time is absolute. At any given moment I am either around whole and entire or I have ceased to be altogether. (Perhaps God will never extinguish my being in fact, but he could do.) There is no sense for the Cartesian in which there might be some individual in the future who was in some respects the same person as I am, and in other respects a different person. Persons are unlike physical things or social organizations in this respect. It is very easy to think of a case where a building (after extensive alterations) is describable as not exactly the same building as, and not exactly a different building from, one which existed on this spot before. (The great cathedrals are often examples of this.) Similarly with a social institution like a club, or indeed a nation. For Nietzsche this kind of thing would be quite possible with individuals, indeed as we age this is just what happens – we gradually change into something which is only in a very slight degree the same individual in any useful sense as that it stems from. More strikingly, Nietzsche insists that even at any one given time there need be no definite single ego. A man (or woman – but Nietzsche on the whole only refers to these as such in order to abuse them) is typically a chaos of opposing wills, each of which has its own aims, and which struggle against one another for mastery of the body.

There is surely a lot of sense in what Nietzsche is saying in this connection. Apart from striking cases of disassociation, most of us really have a variety of different personas, with different, often opposing aims, who take turn to dominate our bodies, or sometimes do not take turn but have a tug of war at one and the same time. Yet there is also what is usually called the unity of consciousness, of which Nietzsche seems to take little account. For, after all, the trouble with these different personas is precisely that they belong to the same stream of consciousness, even within one single moment of the temporal stream, so that they are felt together in one single experience. If this were not so, the position would be less tragic, or tragic in a different way (if, say, one's individual consciousness just ceased for a time and one's body was taken over by a zombie who mucked up one's plans).

I have been sketching something of Nietzsche's views of the nature of reality. In the case of most philosophers one can take it that their theory of reality is meant to be true in some rather objective sense. But Nietzsche expressly maintains that each person has his own perspective on reality, but that there is no independent reality beyond what is presented in the perspectives in terms of which one is more correct than another. If this is so, then it seems that Nietzsche's account of reality as a system of innumerable conflicting wills of power should be taken as just his personal perspective on things, not something which he would want to set up as the one true view of things.

However, the doctrine of perspectivism is presented in terms which really presuppose this view of things, and does not seem to leave this view, therefore, as just one among many ways of conceiving things all possessed of equal right. For what he claims, in advocating perspectivism, is that there is no real world, only the world as it appears to some particular process of willing. A will makes its world out of the raw material of the senses, which may be in various degrees malleable or recalcitrant to its purposes; still, the world which that willing makes is its own work of art, and one which is an essentially free creation, not a portrait to be judged by some criterion of photographic likeness, since there is nothing really there of which it is a portrait. As to where this material provided by the senses really comes from, it is something produced within that centre of will as its particular way of responding to the action upon it of other wills.

Much of this is close to certain forms of idealism. However, Nietzsche rejected any such label. One reason why the label 'idealism' would be particularly unattractive to him would be that idealists are usually thought of as representing the priority of mind in the order of things, while Nietzsche put particular emphasis on the role of bodily processes in determining the course of our mental life. Sometimes this aspect of his thought is referred to as 'physiologism', and it links him again with Schopenhauer. For both of them our consciousness is at the mercy of drives stemming from bodily processes of which we know little, and though both of them also gave a metaphysical interpretation of what the body really is, a system of processes of will, which make of the body itself a kind of low-grade type of psychical or mental reality, the crucial fact is that the aspects of mind on which we peculiarly pride ourselves are the by-products, over which we have little control, of alien processes of no great dignity. Nietzsche, in particular, emphasized the extent to which the general views of the world at which we arrive, after what we think of as careful abstract reasoning, are really just ways, at least very often, of satisfying the instinctive drives of the body. (Both Schopenhauer and Nietzsche anticipated many of Freud's interpretations of systems of ideas along these lines.) The idea that our world picture is largely determined unconsciously in this manner seems somewhat contrary to the idea that we create it by an exercise of our personal will to power. However, his view seems to be that with sufficient determination we can impose the picture we want upon the cosmos, and that in any case whether we impose it on the cosmos or it is imposed on us by our body, it cannot be evaluated for its correspondence with any independent reality which it is supposed to represent, but only for the assistance it is to us in living a fulfilling life.

In the light of this it might seem, then, that Nietzsche's own vision of the world as a battle of individual centres of will to power was not meant to be taken as purportedly literally true in some impossible way, but only as a life-enhancing vision which can help us impose our own will on things. However, since this whole conception of perspectivism is so rooted in his conception of will to power, in myriad different instances, as the essence of reality, it is difficult not to take it as supposed to be in some sense the real truth of things. Or perhaps we can compromise by saying that the view that will to power is the essential motivation of human beings, and the conception of the rest of the universe as also consisting of will to power, is advanced as a kind of myth, which may well be literally true, but the main point of which is to promote the fulfilment of will to power in those who look at the universe in terms of it.

Certainly the main motivation of Nietzsche's thought is to arouse people to the need for a radically new system of values by which to steer their lives, to what he calls a 'transvaluation of values'. His message here is not, it would seem, directed to mankind at large, but to those capable of profiting from it, those who in ways we shall be considering are strong human beings rather than weak ones.

This message has a negative side, and a positive one. On the negative side his aim is to make people fully aware of what in their heart of hearts they really know in any case, but are reluctant to face up to, that 'God is dead'. Sometimes this is presented as though it were the very heart of his philosophy.

When Nietzsche says that God is dead he means that the age has now arrived when belief in God has either been abandoned, or is kept up as a kind of surface belief which is discounted at the deeper levels of our being which determine how we really feel about life. Nietzsche, of course, thinks that the belief in God is false, yet in terms of his perspectivism it would seem to be his view that it did once play a part as a myth which could enhance our lives for us, but that it has now utterly lost that power, and lingers on merely as a refuge from facing up to what we need to do with our lives in a universe we recognize to be godless. Nietzsche thinks that we live in an age of despair, because we still think of value and significance in life as something which must derive from some source outside ourselves. We can only save ourselves from despair, from what Nietzsche calls nihilism, by some radically new approach to the whole question of values and morality.

I speak of Nietzsche's belief about *our* age, although he was writing about a hundred years ago, because I imagine that he would think we are still living in essentially the same historical epoch. However, the hundred years which have elapsed since then may make one wonder whether he exaggerated the extent to which man needed some radically new system of values in order to escape from the despair which atheism would otherwise produce. For there seem to be innumerable people who do not believe in God, and who, without passing through any great gulf of despair, seem to live on moderately contentedly with a system of values, give or take a few changes, such as a permissive sexual ethic, not so different from that of the run-of-the-mill Christian of Nietzsche's time.

Nietzsche might point to some of the great horrific turmoils of the twentieth century as evidences of an underlying despair. In his own country Nazism might be seen as a desperate and catastrophic search for new values. The main point to emphasize, however, is that Nietzsche thought that atheism could be either of a more superficial or of a deeper sort, and that superficial atheism is a dodge to escape the terrifying challenge of the latter. The superficial atheist says that there is no God, but he continues to think that things have intrinsic values, that some kinds of behaviour are better than others, some activities more and others less worth while, in a manner which is not determined by human decision. But this is just what is impossible, according to Nietzsche, if the universe is not the product of any kind of plan on the part of a cosmic mind. Once you really take in the fact that the world is godless, you will realize that things are simply there as sheer pointless matter of fact, and that there is nothing worth while, good or bad about them. It may take ages before many men really face up to this fact, and until they do they will have a submerged sense that there is nothing which really matters in the universe. This will spoil their joy in living, but, since they have not consciously identified it as a problem, they will not be able to do anything about it. The essence of the transvaluation which Nietzsche urges is that we must learn to enjoy the passing moment in its ephemeralness in a really deep way, for the value we charge it with by our own act of will, and not because it points to some world beyond in which the true realization of value must lie, as Christianity, and most metaphysical systems, teach. But let us take a look at Nietzsche's new table of values in more detail.

The first thing to make clear is that there are two very different human types, whom we may call the strong and the weak. We should not think that the same system of values is appropriate for both types, and Nietzsche's system is essentially directed to the strong, or at least those who have some potentiality for making themselves strong. The weak will not grasp the significance of his thought, so that readers who go along with him can take it that they are of the elect.

If we look back to the origins of systems of morality and of value in the Western world we discern a world in which the dominating value system was that of the strong. It is this value system which is imprinted in the language of the ancient Greeks, for whom the antithetical terms were not good and evil in a modern sense, but good and bad in a sense where these corresponded to noble and ignoble. Goodness, as nobility, did not consist in goodness in the modern sense of unselfishness and compassion, but in such qualities as courage, self-respect, determination not to brook injury. Goodness consisted in personal achievement and power, it included even the possession of wealth, but above all it was a matter of personal prowess. There was nothing essentially other-directed about it. The good man lived for himself.

This was then the primary value system, in terms of which men graded themselves and each other. However, there tended also to be a secondary value system applied to inferiors, both by themselves and by their superiors, according to which inferiors gained marks for their serviceability to the noble ones. The qualities which constituted a man good in this secondary sense were more like what have tended to be listed as virtues in the conventional moralities of modern times, such as loyalty, unselfishness, and above all obedience to superiors. The weak who exhibited these qualities in their dealings with the strong gained their protection. Nor, seen from the point of view of the dominant value system of those days, was the praise of the weak for the possession of such qualities as these a mere hypocrisy. These were qualities on which the weak could intelligently pride themselves, for in so far as they realized that real worthwhileness was found only in the lives of those they allowed to be their masters, they could ascribe a genuine instrumental value to themselves as helping these to live their lives to the full. Thus they could earn for themselves a kind of genuine reflected glory.

Gradually, however, there came about a change, for the weak found they could infect the strong with something of the system of values by which the weak themselves were evaluated, as a system for evaluating human worth in general. They managed to make the strong feel that in truth they were inferior to the weak, so that the strong became ashamed of their own virtues and even came to think that their proper task was to use their superior powers to tend the weak.

The crucial point in this development was the arousal of the feeling of pity in the strong, together with a sense that this feeling, and the actions of assistance to which it prompts, is of higher value than joy in one's own talents. Pity, so I take it Nietzsche holds, is an inevitable tendency of human nature, since psychological mechanisms of association are bound to make signs of suffering in others arouse sympathetic suffering in the observer. That it is natural, however, does not of itself count in its favour, and in the heyday of the value system, whose going under we are describing, it was regarded as a weakness which would distract from doing anything worth while. Still, its naturalness means that an appeal to the values which the impulse of pity fosters is bound to have some force, and the weak exploited this, so that the strong lost the capacity to enjoy a life devoted to the development of their own powers, and increasingly saw it as their role to serve the community in general, in which, of course, the weaklings were in the majority. This meant that a gradual transformation overtook society in which control passed to those who had the qualities typical of those who used to be the inferiors in society.

The greatest victory ever won by the weak over the strong came with Christianity, whose gospel of meekness and humility and love is an intoxicating celebration of the importance of the weak, the second-rate, the mediocre. It was, of course, originally the religion of an oppressed race, and then of slaves, in short, of people who are either in a low station through weakness or weak through their low station. It took a long time for the cringing values represented by Christianity really to replace the old values, but with the triumph of humanitarian movements in modern times it is moving towards its logical conclusion, a state of society in which the main resources of humanity go to tending the feeble-minded and sick, who can contribute little to the development of human excellence. In a modern society, dominated by the humanitarian sentiment which is the chief legacy of Christianity, the weak have, in effect, become the strong. As individuals they remain weak and pathetic, but as a group they have come to dominate those who would otherwise be (and whom we may continue to call) the strong, whose energies are either sapped by guilt feelings and pity or devoted to the relief of suffering. Thus are the strong deflected from promoting that which alone gives point to existence, the development of all forms of human excellence.

In a Christian society, or in a humane society dominated by a secular residue of Christian morality, that which is admired most is a kind of tepid harmless way of life in which no individual sets himself up against another as in any way better, and in which there is an absence of strong passions. People of a more vigorous disposition are only tolerated if their energies are devoted to welfare work on behalf of the tepid majority, or those incapable of even such achievements as pertain to these, such as the physically and mentally sick. People with vigorous natures, who might be able to excel in any way, are made to feel ashamed of any pleasure they take in their own talents, and can only rid themselves of such shame by service to others, to the weak. Thus the weak have found a splendid way of arranging things to suit their own dispositions. The qualities, such as a readiness to obey without falling out of line, which originally had a value in inferiors who could thereby assist superiors in doing something worth while, without being a trouble to them, have become part of an armoury whereby the natural servants become masters exploiting the pity of those who have any real forcefulness of nature.

The feebleness of passion of the weak is celebrated as a virtue partly in order to make the strong feel ashamed of the urges which might lead them to, as it would be put, exploit other people. Such weakness of passion is represented as a victorious act of self-control, while in fact it is mere fear of getting into trouble, or perhaps an actual lack of intrinsic vigour. However, there are some other aspects to the whole ethics of self-control, with asceticism as its ultimate development, on which Nietzsche has some interesting things to say.

It is to be noted first that self-control will be a high value even, indeed especially, among persons whose ideal is some form of personal excellence. One can only develop great talents by iron self-discipline. Here, however, what is controlled is the disorganized mass of passions which stand in the way of some great master passion achieving its goals. This is different from the appearance of self-control on the part of the weak who refrain from doing anything much with their lives from timidity. It is also different from another kind of asceticism which has grown up in the Christian era, where there is a persistent effort to damp down one's whole passionate nature, as a way of avoiding suffering. This type of asceticism was the dominant motif in Buddhism. Yet Buddhism arose among those who had grown weary of a life too rich, and is therefore in a manner a final phase in the development of strong natures, while

Christian asceticism represents a flight from suffering on the part of the constitutionally weak.

Thus some of the religious disciplines associated with Christianity as an organized religion have had a limited value, in terms of Nietzsche's own moral system, in creating traditions of self-control and asceticism which we may benefit from when we have thrown off all the corrupting and debilitating aspects of Christian belief and practice. But though Christianity has aspects which have helped prepare man for the development of fresh forms of human excellence, it is for the most part a drag upon such development and the time has come for men of any quality to throw off its shackles. The pressing need is to free ourselves, not so much from the system of beliefs about God, an after life, and so forth, which have come to look so ridiculous to most of us that they need not be the cause of much concern, as from the Christian sense of values. We must free ourselves from the thought that our first task must be to relieve suffering and to work for forms of political organization which will promote the greatest happiness of the greatest number. This for two reasons. First, if there is anything which makes human life worthwhile it is not that some large number of thoroughly mediocre individuals should pass through so many decades of life in a state of moderate contentment. Such lives might just as well never occur for all real point they have. No, the one thing which can make the existence of the human race something in which a thoughtful man can take satisfaction is that certain of its members reach the heights of human excellence. And this brings us to the second reason why the quest to eradicate all removable suffering is an unacceptable ideal for Nietzsche, namely that without great suffering there can be no great excellence. In the end the truly developed human being will know great joy, but his path to it will be through all sorts of suffering which we should not try to remove. Thus we should not waste time on relief of the suffering of those botched efforts of nature which most human beings are, and those who are capable of developing into really worthwhile human beings should not be hamstrung by pity for the masses; and we should not try to make life easy for those capable of becoming something worth while, for this will frustrate their self-development.

Nietzsche's message is directed at single individuals with the capacity to make something of it, and is not primarily conceived as the basis for any political programme. Yet it is of interest to ask what kind of political position it is calculated to inspire. The one political party which officially endorsed Nietzsche as one of its inspirations was German Nazism. It is still hotly debated whether this could only be done by sheer perversion of his thought, or whether something like Nazism is its true logical consequence. The truth seems to be that in certain respects the two come very close, but that there are also enormous divergences. One divergence much insisted on by Nietzsche's (non-Nazi) supporters is that Nietzsche was passionately opposed to the anti-semitic movements which were burgeoning in his day. In fact, he held that the proper breeding of the really good Europeans of the future would include the Jewish strain as an essential ingredient. The reader will realize that though this fact certainly dissociates Nietzsche from the anti-semitism of which, one regrets to say it, his master Schopenhauer was guilty, as also his one-time friend Richard Wagner, it lets the cat out of the bag that Nietzsche sometimes looked forward to state-organized breeding directed at development of the species, and though this was rather an idea he sometimes played with than a central plank in his thought, it has a Nazi air about it.

But even if Nazism has Nietzschean elements in it, it would be wrong to think that this of itself is the condemnation of Nietzsche, since evil systems may owe their success partly to their being corrupt versions of what can command a decent man's assent. It is more appropriate to draw connections between his thought and the outlook of Conservative politicians of the type who oppose socialism and the welfare state as molly-coddling people in a way which stunts enterprise, and comprehensive schools as holding back those of real ability for the sake of sustaining a quite spurious sense of human equality. The British reader may be intrigued by the fact that Enoch Powell, before he became a Christian, appears to have regarded himself as a Nietzschean.

There is, however, a great difference between Nietzsche's ultimate ideal and that of many of the Conservative politicians (really *laissez-faire* liberals), who stress the value of competition and individual initiative, and wish to reduce reliance on a maternalistic welfare state. For often these politicians tend to be what we have called 'washing-machine materialists', who have no other clearly envisaged end in view beyond the ever-increasing production and consumption of material goods, cars, television sets and videos. Nietzsche would have been as contemptuous of this as of the humanitarian ideals of socialism, despising both for setting up a kind of bovine comfort as the real goal, even if for the Conservative the means to this comfort is struggle in the market place. Indeed, the kind of socialism which concerns itself with providing the public with what it ought to want, rather than with what it does want, might be nearer to Nietzsche's heart – he would surely have preferred a state monopoly of television directed to lifting the national consciousness to higher things, as in Britain Labour politicians did, than commercial television providing easy pap. Perhaps in the end a non-sadistic type of Fascism, with policies designed to pick out the really able in all fields for training in self-development, and to give the masses a sense of service and sufficient low-grade happiness to keep them at work for their masters, is the politics a Nietzschean would favour, if he thought it practicable. In general, however, Nietzsche put little trust in governmental promotion of his ideals and thought their pursuit a matter for the solitary individual.

The interpretation I have been offering of Nietzsche's thought makes it look harsher than it appears in the accounts of some exponents. I have suggested that it is a message meant only for a minority, who are bid concern themselves as little as possible with the welfare of the surrounding majority of mediocrities. As against this, it has been suggested that Nietzsche is really addressing every human being who will listen and bidding him (or her, presumably) look to his own strengths and try to develop them, avoiding any temptation to take refuge from this, the true human task, by worrying about the fate of those who make a mess of their lives by lack of determination.

Someone with such an outlook can certainly look to Nietzsche as a stimulus in his quest for self-development, can perhaps even look upon himself as a modified Nietzschean, but Nietzsche himself seems to take the harsher line.

Most people probably associate Nietzsche above all with his idea of the *superman* (*Übermensch*), or, as some prefer to say, as more literal a translation and less likely to invoke memories of comic strips, the *overman*.

When Zarathustra, the spokesman of Nietzsche's ideas in *Thus Spoke Zarathustra*, first comes forward with the doctrine of the superman, he says that 'all beings so far have created something beyond themselves', meaning, it seems, that every other animal but man is to be thought of as a stage towards the development of some further more highly evolved being, and that man should regard himself as similarly possessing value only as a bridge between some kind of ape and something superior to himself. He says also that the greatest experience we men can have is that of 'the great contempt', in which we realize what half-baked creatures we are and see ourselves as without justification unless as due to develop into something higher. This great contempt is, however, quite different from the self-contempt the Christian is expected to have for himself as a sinner. In the latter case one is ashamed that one's desires are tied to earthly things, rather than heavenly, whereas Zarathustra urges us to 'remain faithful to the earth' and see the natural world as the only genuine reality and therefore the only possible domain in which we can find any purpose for our existence. It is, indeed, essentially our inability to give ourselves fully up to joy in earthly existence which marks us as something which should give way to a better constituted creature. Since we have not the force to live a life which is self-justifying through the zestful employment of our own powers, we should see our main task as that of so living and organizing things that a less guilt-ridden and more richly endowed being should emerge. (This aspect of Nietzsche's thought was a main influence on Bernard Shaw.)

It is not too easy to grasp what we may best do to promote the arrival of the superman, nor what his characteristics will really be. Apart from this, there seems a certain tension between two Nietzschean messages, the first that we should regard the present time, and our own existence, as of no value in itself, but only a means to producing a higher kind of existence in some hereafter of the earth's history, and the second that, if we are the kind of people to whom Nietzsche is addressing himself, we should set ourselves to live as vivid and fulfilling a life in the present moment as we can.

The tension can perhaps be resolved if we take it to be Nietzsche's view that it is only in so far as we are incapable of living really worthwhile lives ourselves that we should devote ourselves to preparing the ground for the superman. The best thing is to be a superman oneself, but if this is beyond us, then, just as the herd man will always receive his only, but still a genuine, justification for his being in his service to superiors, so may we, if falling between herd man and superman in our own natures, find our justification for our being in providing the service of *generating him* to the superman. This is not necessarily a matter of procreation, but of contributing to the development of a cultural milieu favouring his development.

Such reconciliation of a seeming conflict between Nietzsche as a philosopher of life in the present and as a philosopher urging us to work for a future we will doubtless not personally even witness demands that we understand the expression 'superman' as referring not to some further species but simply to the ideal human being, and upon the whole this does seem to be his meaning. Indeed, it is doubtful whether it is really very central to his thought to look upon the redeeming of the world from sheer meaninglessness as turning upon the development of supermen in the future, since he sometimes seems scathing about special concern with the future, urging rather that it is really the emergence of superior human beings at odd points throughout historical time, past and future, that should make us feel that human existence is worthwhile

The real difficulty with Nietzsche, I think, is the vagueness of his conception of the really worthwhile human life which a superman might live. He seems to be a proud, somewhat lonesome being, bent on developing his own creative powers without allowing himself to become so overspecialized that he loses his balance as a human being. Great creative artists seem to come nearest to the ideal, provided they do not become too closely identified with just one type of artistic creation. Goethe represented this kind of ideal for Nietzsche. I suspect that Picasso came as near to the superman ideal as anyone has done.

One great test for Nietzsche of a person's approximation to superman status lay in his reaction to a teaching which had for him a strange emotional significance, the doctrine of the eternal recurrence. According to this, the whole process of cosmic history consists in a series of total cosmic events or states of the universe which repeats itself again and again. If, for simplicity, we call a certain state of affairs A, the first event in the series, and think of it as leading up to Z as the last, then Z is followed by an identical A which is followed by an identical series of events leading up once more to an identical Z and so on for ever. There was, in fact, never a first A, for every A followed on a Z which ended a previous series and so on back for ever. Indeed, picking on an event and calling it, under the heading of A, the first of the repeating series would be arbitrary, since we could think equally well of the series as passing through from, say, M to L. So the history of the universe is circular.

Nietzsche offered a supposed proof of the doctrine, somewhat like the following. The world consists of a finite number of particles which, at any moment, are arranged in a certain way in a finite space, and there are only a finite number of possible ways in which they can be arranged, though of course this number is inconceivably large. They shift from one of these arrangements to another according to unvarying laws of nature, or more correctly, in ways determined by the abiding intrinsic potencies of each, acting and reacting on each other. It follows that if the particles ever fall into an arrangement, say X, which they have been in before, their next arrangement will be the same as followed on it last time, and so on till all the arrangements which followed on X the last time round follow on each other again in the same order, ending, of course, with X again, from which the whole series will inevitably follow on once more. Thus if the universe ever repeats the same arrangement twice, it must have a cyclical history of this sort, while that it will fall into the same

110

arrangement twice (and thus infinitely often) is settled by the fact that there are only a finite number of possible arrangements of the particles (not all of which so to speak geometrically possible arrangements need ever figure in the series, but which do not provide enough alternatives for a non-repeating universe).

This is not quite Nietzsche's argument, but sufficiently close to give the reader an idea of the kind of point being made, and exhibiting much the same appeal and weaknesses. One of these weaknesses is that no very compulsive conception of the ultimate constituents of the universe would imply a finitude in the possible systems of relationship in which they can stand to each other. For Nietzsche these constituents are really centres of will to power, not particles, but the point holds almost whatever they are supposed to be. Both in my simplified version and in his the argument sets out from highly doubtful premisses, such as this.

The weakness of the argumentation for the eternal recurrence has sometimes been given as a reason for thinking that Nietzsche took neither argument nor conclusion seriously, not at least as pointing to anything literally true about the universe. Rather, so it is suggested, the whole thing is more by way of being a parable. Yet the argument is not worse than others which have presented themselves to clever men as proofs of positions to which they had some initial inclination, and which they took most seriously, and, until one gets down to details, there *is* something rather persuasive in the idea that the universe must exhaust its possibilities and repeat itself in a manner from which all things will follow on again as previously. Indeed, as a speculation it is not so far-fetched.

The idea has certainly a kind of magnificence about it. There is something vibrant in the thought that, as you sit talking to some loved person on a sunny day in a woodland glade, you are having an exchange which has occurred an infinite number of times before, the same in every detail, and which will reoccur again and again divided by vast stretches of cosmic history in which the solar system plunges to ruin and, epochs later, evolves once more.

Reflection on it raises, however, the question whether the people having this identical conversation at those other times will be us, or different people who are our duplicates. Will *I* have to go through all the same experiences I have suffered in my life, or is it rather that someone else, indeed a succession of others, will have to do so? Some contend that after such a break in consciousness, and without any soul supposed to exist through the interval, it would not be *me* again. Others might rest the issue on whether it was the same 'matter' which made one up, or only similar matter, a question which would only seem to make sense on the supposition that there are permanent particles which endure throughout all time and whose recombination could provide a genuine material identity. For myself, so far as the whole doctrine seems intelligible at all, I think it does amount to the view that we our very selves will be here again doing the very same things again, for it is hard to see what stronger form of survival there might be than to survive with precisely the same character and feelings, perhaps even with the same 'matter' to one's body, and beside these factors the temporal interruption seems to have little weight. This would seem to have been how Nietzsche himself looked on the matter, and though it may at first seem to conflict with his taking a rather dim view of the reality of personal identity throughout one particular life, in fact the two go naturally together, both stemming from treating the identity of the person as a matter of identity of character, rather than of some soul substance.

As to whether Nietzsche thought that the eternal recurrence was a literal truth or not, we have encountered a similar question already regarding his whole doctrine of the will to power as the very essence of all reality, and a similar answer seems right in both cases. We may take it, then, that he thought that the eternal recurrence was very probably true, but that whether it is or not, it is a possibility the dwelling on which is an exercise of one's will to power by which one may test the positiveness of one's own feeling for life.

Nietzsche believed that most people would find the thought of the eternal recurrence quite horrifying, would reflect on all the sufferings experienced by themselves and pitied in others, and would be aghast at the idea that these would come back again and again for ever. It would be welcomed only by one who had known such deep fulfilling joy that he would feel that all the terrible things of his own, and of universal, history could be accepted willingly as elements in the perpetually repeating process to which this joy belonged. For the man who can say this 'yea' to the eternal recurrence realizes that everything is so bound up with everything else that it is either a matter of the whole thing again and again, or none of it, and his joy has been so great that he welcomes the whole thing in spite of all the horrors included in it.

The man who has experienced such joy, and who is thus a yea-sayer to the whole of things, is at, or close to, the level of the superman. Such a man surveys all that he knows of history, and, without any illusions about the nastiness of most existence, recognizes across the ages the existence of men, of whom he himself counts as one, whose creative joy, as they have exercised their will to power, gives what would otherwise be but a sorry affair an ultimate justification. The world was not made with the purpose of producing such men, for the world is just there, it has no purpose, but it is thus justified in the sight of men like him. But most men can only face the suffering essential to existence if they think of this world as somehow leading on to another one, most obviously some after life for men like themselves in Heaven, in which suffering will be abolished and there will be eternal safety.

The idea of the eternal recurrence sounded some deep emotional chord in Nietzsche, and he is at his most eloquent in presenting it. Its true fascination lies, perhaps, in the way it captures a certain eternal quality we half suspect belongs to every passing moment. One may doubt, however, whether it is only people whom we would admire as standing out from the vulgar herd through their personal excellence to whom the idea might appeal. In his play *I Have Been Here Before*, J. B. Priestley presents the theory of time of P. D. Ouspensky, according to which some of us live in a world of such circular eternal exact recurrence, while others of us live in a world which is rather spiral, inasmuch as we can gradually alter things for better or worse when they come round again and again, until we swing out to a better or a worse existence. Such a theory is of doubtful coherence (how can one person have exact repetition if another related to him has shifted things?), but Priestley shows well the way the different possibilities strike different people emotionally, and exhibits a pleasant but very mediocre contented man, nearer to the miller of Dee than a Nietzschean hero, bent on self-overcoming, or a superman experiencing some ineffable depth of joy, as the type who is delighted to hear he will live the same life again and again. That Nietzsche thought the idea so terrifying was, indeed, partly because it came to him primarily as an alternative to the then general belief in an after life for which this was a trial. For people who saw the point of this life in this way, the denial of any world but this, he thought, would be bad enough in itself, but the extra thought that this world would occur again and again, without any point beyond itself, would be appalling to all those who could not make enough for themselves of this life to be pleased to see it given the kind of quasi-eternal status eternal recurrence would give it. So the thought of the eternal recurrence is the litmus test as to whether one has really found joy or not in this life, and Nietzsche was sufficiently imbued with the considerations which lead a Schopenhauer to his pessimism to think that only extraordinarily endowed and courageous beings can pass this test.

Of Nietzsche's five main themes, that God is dead, that man should regard himself as but a bridge to the superman, that the world eternally recurs, that we should recognize will to power as our own essence and that of the cosmos at large and develop a new morality upon this basis, and that pity for suffering should be checked in the interests of self-development, it is the last two which are of most continuing significance. It is hardly intoxicatingly exciting or depressing to be an atheist today; the idea that God may, after all, be alive and well has more excitement for a modern, though it is worth bearing in mind Nietzsche's claim that the denudation of all value from the world except what we give it by our own free choice is a consequence of atheism which is slow to sink in. As genetic engineering gets under way, the idea that it is our role to produce a new race of superior beings may attain a new significance, but the real question will be what sorts of being we value most, and the doctrine of the superman is not of itself especially helpful here. The eternal recurrence hints at a kind of sacredness which belongs to every passing moment if we use it right, but gives little guidance as to how we should fill it. The last two doctrines indicate an approach to life which represents a real challenge to the morality which most people still profess. They tell us that we waste our time if we work to remove suffering from the world, first because we are unlikely to succeed, secondly because most people are so mediocre that it hardly matters much whether their time is passed more or less pleasantly. What really matters is that human life at certain points should reach the heights, and we should not be checked in pursuing this goal in ourselves, or in those whom we can help on, by pity for those who can never do anything of any real value.

This remains a serious challenge to any approach to morality which, like Schopenhauer's, takes compassion as the fundamental quality of the good man. Even if we reject the extreme elitism of Nietzsche's approach, we may still agree that self-development is a task everyone capable of achieving anything much should set themselves, and that this means at least that there is a balance to be struck between concern for oneself and concern for others. Altruism as the sole guide to life is incoherent, since the only thing one could then do for another is give him something to do for oneself, and such taking in of each other's washing leaves nothing for anyone to wear. The ideal of 'the man for others' is an inadequate human ideal, since it presupposes that there is something of value a man can be for himself. However, I do not myself think Nietzsche is especially illuminating as to what a really worthwhile human existence is, or would be, like. I suggested that a great artist like Picasso, vigorous and selfish, is the best exemplar of the Nietzschean ideal. But then we value Picasso in the end for his paintings, not for his painting, which suggests that it may be not so much human self-development as what human beings create or find for their contemplation which matters. There seems a certain failure to recognize this side of things in Nietzsche, as would emerge more fully if we had time to examine his theory of art. This supplies a needful corrective to the Schopenhauerian view of art as merely a kind of quieter of the will, but in its stress upon the zest for life communicated by the best art it lets the work of art itself, as opposed to its effects, fall into the background, something of which our next theorist of existence, Heidegger, made much in his work on Nietzsche.

SIX

HEIDEGGER AND BEING-THERE

The main work of Martin Heidegger (1889–1976) is *Being and Time*, published in 1927. It was, for a long time, regarded as the chief document of the nontheistic wing of that philosophical movement which is known as existentialism. However, Heidegger in later years was anxious to dissociate himself from existentialism, and great as was his influence on Sartre, and much as he himself was influenced by writers usually classified as existentialists, such as Kierkegaard and Jaspers, not only the character of his later work, but the clarification it offers of his aims in his earlier work, make it better to avoid thus designating him.

Heidegger always wrote in a most extraordinary style which is apt to become still more extraordinary in translation. He and his followers claim that the insights he offers us demand the breaking down of familiar ways of speaking and that attempts to expound him in more conventional language can only distort things. One can say, at least, that it will not be easy to get agreement as to what it is that he is asserting once one ceases merely to parrot his own sayings. The reader is warned that in this chapter my interpretations are particularly open to challenge.

Heidegger in his earlier career was a follower of Edmund Husserl (1859–1938). Husserl was the originator of a philosophical movement known as phenomenology. A main theme of phenomenology is that when one wants to understand what some certain sort of thing really is one should throw oneself, really or in imagination, into the sort of mental activity by way of which one normally encounters such things. Whether the question is what numbers are, what physical reality or laws of nature are, or even what mind itself is, one must examine what comes before one in one's ordinary way of concerning oneself with such things, in the case of numbers, for example, by carrying out mathematical calculations and striving to capture in words the precise essence of what then presents itself to the mind. In this way one returns to 'the things themselves', and avoids mere logic-chopping. Phenomenology tends to lead on to some kind of idealism, since its method suggests that what things truly are is no more and no less than what they are for our consciousness. This was an implication Husserl himself, after some early doubts, embraced.

In *Being and Time* Heidegger writes expressly as a phenomenologist, but his method and concerns contrast strikingly with Husserl's. First, his way of going to the things themselves is to consider what they are for us, not primarily in the rather remote study-bound theorizing and perceiving through which Husserl invited them to reveal themselves, but in the hurly-burly of working life and ordinary leisure. Second, he dissociates himself from an essentially Cartesian note in Husserl's thought, on such central topics as mind, consciousness, and scepticism. Third, he lays great stress on what is revealed to us in a certain basic anxiety which lies at the base of our being. Fourth, his whole enterprise is powered by his concern with one fundamental question: 'What is being?'

All of Heidegger's philosophy, in fact, from first to last, is one long meditation upon this question. He contends that man has lost his sense for the importance of this question, and is all agog to know what different beings there are, and what their specific natures may be, but neglects to ask himself what is said and thought concerning them when we say that they *are*. The fundamental question is not what *is* but what it is to *is*.

Way back in antiquity certain great minds, such as Parmenides and Heracleitus, did dwell on this question. In all subsequent philosophy and in human life generally this fundamental question has been forgotten. It is the forgetting to concern oneself with the question which is the source, it seems to be implied, of most of men's troubles. Heidegger endeavours to bring us back to meditation upon this basic question.

That this is his aim is, indeed, stated in *Being and Time*. However, partly for somewhat extrinsic reasons, this work was published in an incomplete form (though it is far from short) and was never finished, and that means that inquiries which are really preliminary to confrontation with the basic question look like the main theme. The question of being is more clearly dominant in later writings.

Sometimes Heidegger seems more concerned to have us meditate on the question than try out answers to it. He seems to feel that there is a certain vulgarity in a ready answer, and that such answers as have been proffered since the days of those early Greeks do not steadily distinguish this question of what being is from questions as to what beings there are. (I do not think he is right about this. Many philosophers have sharply distinguished the question what it is for something to be from any question as to what there is, even if Heidegger would dismiss their answers as grossly inadequate.)

In approaching the question as to what being is, Heidegger proposes that the questioner does best to ask himself what his own being is, what it is for him himself to be. For some inadequately conceptualized sense of what our being is is certainly contained within that being, as also a very special concern with that being, both as to what it is and as to how long it will last. If we manage to bring our own being into a clearer light we may expect the being of other sorts of being than those who thus question their being to catch something of that light too.

The contrast between the being we have and which things have, and other such contrasts indicated in his work, suggest that Heidegger, effectively, takes up a position, on a question philosophers have often debated, somewhat other than what one might at first think, when he invites us to meditate on being itself rather than on the beings which have being. Some philosophers hold that the verb 'to be' ('is', etc.) has the same meaning whatever it is that is said to be. The difference always lies in the character of what *is*, not in what it means to say they *are*. Others say that being means something quite different when quite different sorts of things are said to be. (The very dispute shows that Heidegger misrepresents things in insisting that the question of what being itself is has been forgotten.) One would expect a philosopher who speaks so much and so darkly of being to be in the first group, and often, especially in his later work, he does seem to be. However, such contrasts, as that in question now, imply that his position is that of the second group of philosophers. This, I think, makes it difficult to make sense of the insistence one finds in him that we should get away, as philosophers at least, from attempting to classify the different kinds of being which there are, and ask what their being is, since for the second group of philosophers these questions are scarcely distinguishable. However, we must follow the Heideggerian path as best we can.

The questioner who puts the question 'What is being?' should look, then, first to his own being. But what kind of being asks the question? Is it a man (or woman)? To say so can be misleading, according to Heidegger, for it suggests that the questioner has a being akin to that possessed by things in the world and that we should look to zoology, anthropology, or some other natural science for an understanding of its being. But we know in our hearts that our being is not something to be discovered there. Is it then a pure consciousness, of the Cartesian kind, that is asking itself about its being? We shall see why Heidegger rejects this proposal also. Some new way of referring to that which asks the question is needed, implying neither of these misconceptions.

Heidegger adopts the expression '*Dasein*' to designate the one who asks the question of being. You and I are each a '*Dasein*'. This German word is usually left standing in translations of Heidegger, adding unnecessarily to the general oddness of the text. It seems better to translate it as 'Being-there', which corresponds more or less to the relevant normal meaning of the German word, and is not much odder as a noun. Sometimes, like Heidegger himself, I shall be content to speak more naturally of *man*.

Certain key characteristics of Being-there are explicated at length by Heidegger. I shall mention only a significant selection. First, a characteristic of Being-there which is crucial is what may be called its being-in-the-world. Being-there is not something which has a substantial existence which it could conceivably sustain in isolation from other things. Each individual being-there exists by inhabiting an environment, and it simply makes no sense to try to think of a reality of the same type which does not. That is a main reason for dissociating a correct conception of a Being-there from any Cartesian notion of a mind or consciousness, since that is supposed to be something which could exist and wonder whether it was in a world, something, indeed, which might, in truth, not be in a world at all.

Although being-in-a-world, indeed being-in-the-world, is essential to Being-there, a being-there, like you or I, is not in the world in the sense in which a thing is. The ordinary objects we bump across as we walk about are described by Heidegger (as usually translated) as accessible within the world. If I were expressing similar thoughts on my own account I might speak of ordinary things as being in the world and say that Being-there inhabits a world, but in Heideggerian language, as anglicized, ordinary objects are not in, but within, the world.

Heidegger aims to find a way in which we may characterize ourselves for which we are neither merely organisms within the world, nor pure consciousnesses which animate organisms, nor a combination of the two. But his conception is hard to grasp. Some quite recent British philosophers have made a point of taking persons as constituting a fundamental category, not explicable as bodies plus minds. However, it is clear that as they understand persons, these are physical realities stretched out in space, though this is not all they are. It is unclear, I find, whether for Heidegger an individual being-there can be said to have a weight and height.

Another essential characteristic of a being-there is being-with. Here the German *'mitsein'* is peculiarly expressive. It is not just a brute fact that each being-there finds itself one of many, nor does it make any sense for it to wonder whether there really are any others. Even if as a matter of fact I should become the last human being, being-with would remain an essential mode of my being, for I would implicitly sense myself as belonging to a community of beings capable of mutual communication, one of which might turn up at some point from outer space. The fact that I may mistake a waxwork, say, for a human being like me is neither here nor there. What is certain is that I live in a world in which I may meet others with whom I could communicate, not that I am meeting one of them now.

The next key characteristic of a being-there to which I shall turn is its temporality. It always exists in three modes, as a being with a past, a present and a future. It can never merely be tied up in the present. Just as it is senseless for a being-there to wonder whether it exists in a real world, or in a real community with others, so is it senseless for it to wonder whether it really existed in the past or is moving on to a future. The newborn baby can only come to itself as something with a past. As for death, that is not something which happens in any present but something which lies there in the future awaiting us in a manner which is one of the most crucial aspects of our being. Undoubtedly we will end, but as long as one lives one is reaching forwards towards a future of which at least a fraction is always left. The advice of some sages to live in the present would be dismissed as nonsense by Heidegger, since one only is by projecting oneself forward to a future at which one is aiming, or for which one is waiting, on the basis of a still living past, and one's present is the state of choosing what to do with one's past in order to make what kind of future. The fact that one only is by thus forming projects is expressed by saying that our primordial mode of being is *care* and that being-there is by *existing*, which is here given the special meaning of standing out from one's present situation in an active manner which one determines for oneself.

As just noted, Heidegger lays great stress on the significance of the sense of the impendingness of our own deaths as an essential aspect of our being. My mortality is not something which might have been otherwise. Even if there was *de facto* immortality, in another life, or through extraordinary medical advances, I could not become something of a kind for which cessation would not be an ever-present possibility. Thus finitude or mortality is another essential feature of Being-there, in which it contrasts, for example, with the kind of being God would possess if he was.

As we reflect phenomenologically upon our own being and bring such truths about it to light as these, we also bring to light truths about the being of the things in that world which we inhabit, and which is not cut off from us, since being-in-the-world is part of our essential being.

When we do so we become aware that philosophers have made a tremendous mistake about the nature of the things that are there for us within that world. They have thought of them as physical realities whose essential nature is to fill out a position in space by their possession of certain observable or otherwise detectable qualities. Thinking of this as what these things really are, and as that by which they initially make themselves known to us, they have thought that we then calculate how they can be acted on so as to serve our personal purposes better. It makes no difference to the essential error in this conception which qualities are regarded as objective, and which subjective, whether colour, for instance, is thought of as really there or not. For what is forgotten on this account is that what we really initially experience the things around us as being is things each of which essentially points beyond itself to other things. Thus a thing as I experience it may be a tool which points beyond itself to things I might use it for repairing, or it may be something which is useless in the absence of some other object whose present absence it, so to speak, makes present to me. To take a very simple example. The pillar box I see in the street is not initially experienced as an object of a certain shape, colour, probable weight and so on, but as that in which letters are put and collected by the postman. It is not so much that I have learnt that objects of that shape and colour are used for a certain purpose, but that what is actually sensibly present to me is something whose very essence it is to be a receptacle for letters and a gateway to communication with all ends of the earth. It is not experienced as something filling up its own little position in space, though apt to be put to certain uses, but as something essentially referring to the whole human world in which it figures. And that is true of non-artificial objects also. The sun is seen as warden of our hours.

It is true that by a very special kind of attention I may convert the things around me into mere matter filling up space in different ways. When I adopt this attitude I am on the path to science, and questions occur to me, if I am only half inquisitive, as to what this filling up of space is in its finer details, and how they act on each other, questions I must look to scientific inquiry for an answer to. But scientific inquiry is only one way of comporting oneself to the world, and it is a mistake to think that our ordinary experience of the world is grafted on to a more basic way of experiencing things as mere objects it is for science to explain. And even if it is not supposed that the theoretical gaze which lies at the base of science represents our primordial apprehension of the world, it is still a mistake to think that it is only when we adopt it that we come to things as they really are. It is rather in ordinary human practice that we encounter them in their true being.

Heidegger made a famous distinction between the ready to hand and the present at hand, the former being what we encounter around us when we see things in it as essentially related towards all other things with which they come together in human life, the second what we encounter when we denude what lies around us of all human meaning. (The phrase 'ready to hand' suggests, deliberately, the belonging together with other things as administering to human purposes, but if we take into account his later thought it is better to use it so as to cover all kinds of human meaningfulness.) Things belonging to the ready to hand world are in their inner being constituents of a total 'world' the character of which they capture even when seen in their single being, while the things of the present at hand are isolated from each other, acting only upon each other according to laws of nature which are mechanical and meaningless. Or we can put it otherwise, and say that they belong together in the world of scientific thought, which is just one rather specialized world, not the one and only one, or even the most important.

There are various things with which one might take issue in all this, but the thing which is particularly striking is the tendency to identify that which things are for us in our most usual avocations with what they really are. The materialist, or any dualist realist about the physical world, will hold that however specialized an interest scientific inquiry may be, it is there alone that the true character of the world around is, or at least one day may be, limned. Idealists may well see the matter differently, and say that the only real world is the world as it is for us. They might then accept that Heidegger has advanced our sense of what this real world is, adding to it, or rather leaving it with, not only like Berkeley the secondary qualities of which a Locke would purge it, but also its multiple levels of human meaning – something I think already done in some part by Bradley and others. That suggests that we can only make sense of his claims if put in an idealist context. That is fine, but it shows that he has sided in, not, as is often claimed, transcended, traditional philosophic disputes like those between realism and idealism.

Let us turn back to Being-there and consider the rather striking ques-

122

tion which Heidegger poses as to who, in each case, this being-there is. Who is it who is there as you pay for your ticket on the bus, or exchange the time of day politely with your neighbour?

Heidegger's answer is somewhat sinister. Most of the time it is not an authentic individual who speaks and acts, but '*das Man*' in one of its particular actualizations. '*Man*', like the French '*on*', means 'one' in the sense in which one says that this is how one behaves on these occasions. '*Hier spricht man Deutsch*' is a notice at some barbers' shops for which I always wish was substituted 'Here one speaks not at all', as one who finds speaking to barbers an effort. The main translations of Heidegger use 'the they' as a translation of '*das Man*', and one sees that it avoids the suggestion which 'the one' might carry that we have to do with the cosmic consciousness of a monistic metaphysics, but it is misleading too, since when Heidegger speaks of *das Man*, it is to refer to some kind of average mass man of our society which lives in each of us, whereas 'they' is used in English usually to refer to a kind of annoying anonymous quasi-bureaucracy which runs things without *one's* personal consent.

So most of the time what gives itself out as a distinct individual is just a particularization of a standard way of thinking and acting, which, because it is no particular person's decision that it should be as it is, it is no particular person's responsibility to take responsibility for. Moreover, the fact that normally one is merely the one means that one does not face up to personal finitude. One dies, that is to say that persons die, but to realize that one dies is not to realize that this quite personal I will die.

To live as a particularization of the one is to live inauthentically. Heidegger insists that his language here is not morally loaded. Of course, and inevitably, the norm is that one lives normally, thus inauthentically, and authentic existence, in which I assert myself as I myself, with a unique death which I shall suffer alone and no one can die for me, is bound to be the exception which occasionally raises itself above this common level. Yet whatever he says, it is difficult not to see *Being and Time* as a summons to each of us to take responsibility for our lives, and face our deaths, as unique single individuals, free to make of our lives what we freely determine upon. Here we have a theme which is still more central in Sartre, though he rejects the special place assigned by Heidegger to consciousness of death.

There are three things which particularly summon one, or rather dismiss the one and summon up the I, to authenticity. There is the sudden confrontation with the inescapable personal mortality which is my own.

There is anxiety in the face of the nothing. And there is conscience, which comes as the pure call of the I.

We have seen that mortality or finitude is built into each individual being-there as of deep necessity. To grasp this is to grasp that one has a limited time in which either to flounder or make something determinate and unalterable of one's life. Suddenly realizing this, one may be forced to a positive determination of one's being, rejecting the moulding of one's life style by others.

Facing up to nothingness is something we do in anxiety. Suddenly we feel something which is not fear about any particular thing, but a realization that all that is is hung over an abyss of nothingness. The Heideggerian treatment of the nothing is both famous and notorious. In it he stresses the inadequacy of ordinary logic to register the relevant point, which is that the only alternative to there being things at all is nothing, and that that neither does nor doesn't mean that there is no alternative to the being of things, since the alternative which there is is one which is nothing. This negative alternative to there being anything is the dark side of all reality, and we tremble when we realize that there is nothing to prevent all things fading like Prospero's insubstantial pageant or even to explain why they have ever had being at all. In this notion of the nothing is also included, I think, the possibility of a fading away of that whole system of meanings which make a world for us, and in which things alone have their being, a fading away which certainly comes with death but may even come before it, so far as we think of death as a mere event occurring at a certain date.

As for conscience, Heidegger thinks that the phenomenon so called is a coming to me of the sense that it is after all for me to choose and not for one to do what one does. It is interesting that this is just the opposite of the conception of conscience of some sociologists as the voice of society within the individual.

Just as the individual can hear the call to authenticity and recognize that it is for him to determine on his own projects by a creative use of his past, so may a nation. In neither case is it a call to free oneself from one's past (I am no longer using 'one' in a Heideggerian play on words) but to use that past positively. In this connection Heidegger speaks of one's past as lying in the future, meaning that tradition is something to which one must give ever fresh meanings. But when this sort of thing is said of nations we seem to have moved into a different sort of philosophy. Can nations choose? The idea is, presumably, that many individuals with the same historical roots come to maturity in unison in what they make grow therefrom. But there is a certain tension between collectivism and individualism in Heidegger's thought, shown also in his treatment of *mitsein* which seems both a concept of human solidarity and of the way in which the individual grows up weighed down with the interpretations of the world of others.

Our unease is naturally greater still when we contemplate the fact that Heidegger, not, it seems, under pressure, joined the Nazi party in 1933, and remained in it for ten months, having voiced his enthusiasm for its revival of the German nation in published writings, while whether with or without his consent the dedication of *Being and Time* to the Jewish Husserl, who had died in retirement in Switzerland, was removed from new editions. The significance of these sad facts is much disputed. After the war, Heidegger appears to have kept a canny silence. What speaks for him is his continuing friendship with his extremely anti-Nazi one-time student, and mistress, Hannah Arendt, and the general tone of his philosophy, the call of which for personal authenticity and against mass man is hardly totalitarian in character.

This personal folly, from which he drew back, if not with any great bravado, as the Nazi plot thickened, does make one wonder whether he was personally quite the sage his admirers seem to think him, but it is better to hold one's judgement in suspense unless prepared to research the matter in a thorough way, as I have not. So let us think of Heidegger as a great proponent of the significance of personal resoluteness, without deciding on his own relation to the call of conscience.

There is a definite change of tone in Heidegger's later work. The continual meditation on the question of being intensifies, while the emphasis on the authenticity of personal decision decreases. Rather are we beckoned, in a prose which has become something of great beauty, to act as shepherds of being, to let beings be. (This is not the only Heideggerian phrase which chimes in oddly with some of the favourite expressions of our recent popular culture.)

The thought in these later writings is obscure, indeed, but it seems that man or being there is seen as a kind of sunlit clearing in a forest into which beings come, from out of the thickness of the forest or dug up from the earth, in order thereby to become for the first time truly themselves by entering into the light of being.

The relation to idealism seems clearer now. There is a dark realm of reality, the surrounding forest, or the earth below the clearing, in which things lie hid in an undistinguished mass, but they are not individual things with natures until brought into the clearing. As being-there brings them into the clearing of light which is what he truly is, this dark mass sorts itself out into realities, which, for the first time, really are something, and, therefore, for the first time *are*. Thus man gives them being, though he does not create them out of empty air.

They can only acquire their individuality and their being in this clearing which is man because they come to play a part in a human world of meanings. On the other hand, the human worlds into which they can be introduced vary in character and some bring out the being of beings, and let it develop in the fashion proper to it, while others cover things over in a fashion which distorts their individuality rather than merely keeps it in the darkness of the 'earth' – or in the surrounding 'forest'. For although they have no definite being in the 'earth' or 'forest' there is something somehow there ready rather to become one thing than another. Now, some human worlds help bring things to themselves, while others prevent their particular natures from showing themselves and thereby being. A civilized life of harmonious involvement with nature, in which the character of different sorts of raw material is respected and nature is cooperated with rather than exploited, is a world of the first sort, while a world in which man imposes himself upon his environment without any sense of the values and possibilities of harmony between natural things and each other, and himself with them all, is a world of the second sort.

Clearly, Heidegger's feelings are those which inspire the ecological movement, and such organizations as the Friends of the Earth. Whether he has anything very precise to say as to what is exploitation and what is respectful use is not so clear. Presumably the reduction of this to a mere technological question as to what practices threaten the human species with seriously destructive pollution would be thought by him inadequate, since it is precisely the technological approach to nature that he regards as the menace. The human race should stand to nature rather as a sculptor or carver who works with rather than against the wood or stone, helping to display its inherent nature. Heidegger describes beautifully how the architecture of the Greeks, by its construction and placing, or the simplicities of a peasant life of toil, did this for nature, while modern technology, in his eyes, covers the being of nature over – but not in that original darkness for which, as the sacred source of those beings which it is for being-there to bring into the light, it should have reverence as something it will never fully penetrate, but in an artificial and distorting darkness of man's own.

These attractive attitudes fall in with a view of truth peculiar to Heidegger and, if he is right, the earliest Greeks. Truth is usually thought of

126

as the correspondence of a judgement with that which it is about. But Heidegger sees the proper character of truth as captured in the Greek word *aletheia*, which originally meant *uncoveredness*. Thus when things come into the light of human awareness, or should we say more safely, being-there, they are themselves the truth, for they are *being itself* uncovered and illuminated, and this truth which the beings then themselves are is more basic than the truth of any report about them. Truth, moreover, we are told by Heidegger, is the same as human freedom, for freedom lies in our capacity to reveal being appropriately, and the same also as the beauty which reveals things in their own essential being.

But though Heidegger rejects the idea of truth as correspondence of a verbal statement with what it is about, he is far from separating truth from language. For it is in human speaking that we live the life which brings beings into the light of illuminated being. This is true, above all, in genuine poetry where the fuss and bother of ordinary business and chatter fall away and language quietly reveals in a manner which is at once a calling into being. Heidegger, if I may use the old myth here, thinks of creatures as having been given their natures by Adam's first act of naming them, and of the poets as intensifying this original naming and calling forth.

I have sought in this brief presentation of Heidegger's thinking to steer a middle path between use of his own mysterious way of putting things, and a more down to earth manner which would certainly be rejected by his admirers as a travesty. As to the real value of his thought I have no settled judgement to offer, though I do suspect that he and his admirers exaggerate the novelty of much that he has to say. Many of the themes of his earlier work are taken up and developed in the existentialism of Sartre, to which we turn next. Sartre, however, quite lacked the later Heidegger's concern with man's need to rediscover his role as the light of the non-human world.

[SEVEN]

SARTREAN EXISTENTIALISM

This chapter is concerned with the existentialist philosophy of Jean-Paul Sartre as set out in the middle period of his development, especially in *Being and Nothingness* (1943). In his earlier writings Sartre developed a version of phenomenology (the philosophical point of view, touched on in the previous chapter, associated with the German philosopher Edmund Husserl), while in his later writings he developed a kind of existentialist version of Marxism, continuous with the existentialism of his middle period, but diverging from it also in important ways. It would be impracticable to attempt to describe the positions Sartre put forward in his earlier and in his later philosophy as well as giving some account of his middle period, and as it is in the latter that he develops the kind of theory of existence which it suits the character of this book to deal with, I shall confine myself almost entirely to that.

In our first chapter we discussed Cartesian dualism. Sartre is the most decidedly dualist of major philosophers of this century. There are for him two basically different kinds of being, the 'in-itself' and the 'for-itself'. The former is unconscious physical reality, the latter is consciousness. The in-itself does not exist from its own point of view, for it has no point of view, while the for-itself does exist from its own point of view, and is also that from the point of view of which the in-itself exists. Yet though the only being from whose point of view the in-itself exists is the for-itself, Sartre holds that the in-itself exists in itself quite apart from its presence to consciousness or the for-itself, and when, therefore, there is no point of view on it.

Although the in-itself can exist even when it is not present to any consciousness, there is a sense in which as just existing there it has no definite character and does not divide up into definite individual things. Such character and articulation it only has for a consciousness which confronts it with distinctions and contrasts which reflect its own individual purposes. Apart from this, the in-itself is a kind of undifferentiated plenum. It is not even properly speaking temporal; distinctions such as that between past and future depend on consciousness. When, to put it so, there is a change in the in-itself, the new state of affairs does not have a past, and is out of all sort of relation to the previous state of affairs. Only consciousness has a past, for consciousness is laden through memory and guilt and so forth with what it has been. Likewise all characterizations of things in terms of the potentialities they include, and this is perhaps true of all our characterizations of things, have no real application to the in-itself as it is apart from its presence to a consciousness. Clouds do not contain the possibility of rain until a consciousness grasps a connection between them and envisaged rain; all that is true is that the present cloudy sky either is or is not followed by rain – and even this is not really true since clouds, rain and before and after are only there for a consciousness which grasps the relevance of the in-itself to its own purposes.

In all this, Sartre takes up a position, which one may either think subtle or think incoherent and unstable, mid-way between realism and idealism. Something is there apart from its presence to consciousness, but characterization of it as it is in itself is impossible. The trouble, as it seems to me, is that this must be as true of the suggestion that it is somehow undifferentiated, as of any suggestion that it is differentiated according to schemes of division of ours. Moreover, the idea that it is somehow timeless because its past is not still somehow there in its present, as is true in the case of consciousness, is hardly satisfactory, since it is evident that Sartre is not really denying that it changes, and this surely makes it temporal. Yet there certainly does seem a sense in which each of us may make a different world out of what is in some sense the same portion of being (quite apart from straight error), and that there is, therefore, really no world there, until a conscious being creates a system of things in relation (reflecting its own purposes, and in which things divide, for example, into means and ends) from out of that blank being it is in the midst of.

It may be noted that the Sartrean view that each human consciousness makes its own world out of a somehow undifferentiated plenum of being to which it is present, seems to have little or nothing to do with reflections on the way in which the character of our sense organs and brains determines what we make out of the external stimuli affecting us. Sartre seems to think in terms of a much more direct confrontation of consciousness with the world it is in. There is no suggestion that what we know immediately are only some kind of mental representations created within us in response to external stimuli. As against that kind of ground for contrasting the phenomenal world with the world of things in themselves, such as we met with in Schopenhauer (and which stems largely from Kant), Sartre stands out as a kind of direct realist for whom consciousness directly apprehends the things in its environment. His point is that this direct apprehension would confront mere blankness if we did not grasp what we confront in terms of its various different relevances to our projects.

One of the most important ways in which the world in which we find ourselves living is characterized in a manner that could not be true of the in-itself as it is apart from consciousness is that it is shot through with negations, with nothingness, as Sartre puts it. In describing my environment at any given time, negative characterizations play an essential role. I am in my office, say, and not on holiday as I was a week ago, it is not yet time to knock off, the person I expected to be present to discuss certain problems which have arisen is not here, and so forth. The absence of the person I expected to be here is a fact about this room as definite and as perceivable as is the presence in it of tables and chairs. Sartre insists, through long and sometimes arresting discussions of particular examples, that we simply could not describe the world we inhabit without referring to absences and lacks as particularly salient aspects of its character. On the other hand, he also insists that it is nonsensical to think that we can think of any such negativities as pertaining to a world which is not illuminated by consciousness. It is, therefore, through consciousness, or, otherwise put, the for-itself, that negation or nothingness comes into the world.

But how could the for-itself bring negation or nothingness into the world if it did not somehow contain nothingness within it? Nothingness comes to the observed world from the observing consciousness, but that consciousness has nowhere else to get the nothingness it inserts into the world than from itself. It must, therefore, 'secrete its own nothingness'.

The reader who feels that such a suggestion can only be a piece of bizarre verbal fireworks has my sympathy – yet he or she should ask themselves whether they find it strange only because it insists on an answer to a question which it is a limitation of ordinary thought to have overlooked. In any case the matter can, I think, be put in a rather soberer fashion.

We need to follow Sartre in distinguishing between external and internal negations. Suppose I am trying to post a letter, then the fact that there is no pillar box in this street becomes, one is almost inclined to say, a positive characteristic of it, though it is not really a positive character but a negative character which is part of its sensible being as it is for me. It is a quite different sort of negative fact about it from such facts as that there is no elephant or no palm tree in the street. Of course, if my projects were otherwise these could have been similarly sensible negative characteristics of it, but as it is they are only characterizations of the street in virtue of the holding of a verbal rule that every possible characterization which might be given of anything whatever is either true of some particular thing or not true of it. Everything whatever is either in the street or not in the street, and every quality whatever either pertains to it or does not, but this is only a mechanical rule of language, and does not mean that the fact that this street is not a cushion, is not homogeneously blue, and does not have the philosopher Spinoza walking along it are salient facts about the street as I experience it, as is its lack of a letter box. This is not a merely external negation, but a relatively internal one.

Yet if there were only nonconscious 'in-itself', and no consciousness or for-itself, all negations would be equally external. In the absence of any for-itself, no part of the in-itself would be more intimately not one thing than it was not another thing, and none of the things it was not would really pertain to what it was in itself. Indeed, to put it paradoxically, in the absence of a for-itself there would be no real fact of all for-itselfs being absent, and there would be no real boundaries distinguishing one thing from another (since boundaries mark off where a thing is from where it is not), but just a dead level of positive being in terms of which all negations true of a thing would be equally relevant and thus all equally without any significant application to it. It is this irrelevance of negation to the being of the in-itself on its own, together with the essential role negation plays in all real characterization of things and division of the world into distinct parts, which is the main reason for saying that without the for-itself the in-itself would not be a genuine world of things.

The absence of a pillar box from the street, or of water from a desert, are in appropriate circumstances internally negative of a part of the in-itself as presented to a for-itself, but since there is no real negation in the in-itself, consciousness cannot have picked up the idea of negation, nothingness or absence from something which confronts it in radical fashion there, and the only other possibility is that it has somehow picked up the idea of it from itself. This it can only do if there is a still more radical sense in which negation is there within itself. This, in fact, is so. When I am consciously without the food or warmth I desire, or when I am *un*happy, these negations are true of me in an internal fashion, that is, one could not say what my consciousness is in its own right, except by referring to these things which it is not or which it is without. They are not external negations one can concoct regarding it, according to a linguistic rule, but absences which haunt what it actually is. If a modern man is without a television set, this is something pertaining to his consciousness as the lack of a television set was not for Napoleon. The internality of these negations to consciousness is more ultimate than the internality of any negations to unconscious observable realities. The street is without a pillar box, and this is an internal negation of the street as it is for me, but I am without somewhere to post my letter, and this is an internal negation of my consciousness as it is for itself, is, one might say, if it did not clash with Sartrean terminology, an internal negation for my consciousness as it is *in itself.* For this reason consciousness, as that where negation belongs intrinsically, and not as an appearance of the thing to something else, is the ultimate home and source of the negation which there is in the world.

We must be clear that negation, for Sartre, is not some kind of illusion. No amount of purely positive statement would ever really tell us what it is for something not to be something. The fact that there is no pillar box in the street is not reducible to such positive facts as that I looked for a pillar box, and found tarmac and empty air, both because the absence of a pillar box 'haunts' the street as a sensible fact about it, and because my looking for something cannot be expressed properly in purely positive language, it being the lack of somewhere to post a letter consciously felt.

Thus negative characterizations of one's consciousness as it is at any particular juncture go to the heart of what it is in a way which is not true of any part of the non-conscious world, and even the most internal negative characteristics of things rest on internal negative facts about a consciousness which confronts them. (This point about the purely positive character of the in-itself as it is in its own right may seem to clash with the view of Sartre that even specific positive assertions about it as such are equally out, and that we can only say such things as that it is what it is. However, this limitation on what may be said about it turns also on its purely positive character, since any specific assertion has a negative element.) But Sartre goes much further than this. Not only is much of what has to be said about someone's consciousness as it is at any moment negative in character, but in the end everything which can be said about it is negative. Consciousness is only characterizable in terms of what it is not, in terms, that is, of what it is not in an internal fashion, in which its failure to be what it is not belongs to it in an intimate fashion quite unlike that in which, say, the not being a tree pertains to a rock.

There are several aspects to this essentially negative character of consciousness. First, there is the fact that consciousness can only be by being the consciousness of something, and that, according to Sartre, consciousness of something is always at the same time the consciousness, on the part of consciousness, of its not being that thing.

In insisting that consciousness is always the consciousness of something Sartre was following the doctrine of a philosopher by whom he was deeply influenced, namely Edmund Husserl, that the most salient fact about consciousness is that it is intentional, which is simply a technical way of saying that it is *of* something. The point may seem somewhat trivial, but it stands in opposition to philosophies which had thought one can understand the human mind best by asking what goes on *in* it, as part of its make up, and that just as a watch tells the time because it is made up of certain parts and is put to a certain use, so the mind could be about or directed towards things because it was made up in a certain way which allowed it to serve a certain purpose. As against this Husserl and other phenomenologists contended that if one tries to see the mind, understood as consciousness, as being of or about things because it is made up in a certain way which can be studied independently of its intentionality, its being of or about something, one will go hopelessly wrong, since there is nothing more basic than this its intentionality. Sartre, in fact, thought that he had purified this Husserlian doctrine of association with residual non-intentional ways of thinking of consciousness which were present in Husserl. In doing so he contends that when I am conscious of something, say the paper on which I am writing and the facts (as I see them) which I am trying to express, there is really nothing to the situation except the paper and the facts and my consciousness as something whose being is exhausted in its particular way of being conscious to itself of its own contrast with this paper and these facts. Any attempt to regard consciousness as a something, as something which is there in addition to the world of which it is a consciousness, ends up by treating consciousness as made up of elements in a way which betrays the insight into its purely intentional nature. In fact, it does not even have an intentional *nature*, it is just the coming into the light of that which it is consciousness of, it itself being nothing other than a conscious distinctness of itself from its objects.

Many people object to this whole approach and insist that what is conscious of things as I walk around, and think, is this human organism which is as much a thing as anything else. For Sartre, however, it is not really the physical organism which is conscious of things, since only physical facts can apply to a physical organism. Rather is it consciousness itself which is conscious of things from a point of view determined by the organism. With this I agree, on grounds much those which a Cartesian would put forward, and perhaps therefore essentially those of Sartre himself, though I would not, in fact, go along with the mysterious doctrine that consciousness is somehow merely a nothingness characterizable only in pregnant negatives.

In elaborating his doctrine of consciousness as a nothingness, Sartre says that the for-itself is not what it is and is what it is not. This formula concerns the relation in which one stands to one's past and future. If asked what I am I might say that I am a university teacher, who lives in a certain city, and so forth. This is all in a manner true, yet it is untrue if it is understood as saying that I am here and now all this, in the sense in which this typewriter is here and now a typewriter. For what the typewriter 'does' at any moment (or what something self-acting in a more positive way, such as a plant, 'does' at any moment) springs from its being a certain definite sort of something, which one would try to catch in saying what it is. However, I only deceive myself if I think that what I am doing here and now follows from all the things I might say that I am, in this same mechanical or quasi-mechanical fashion. All that I might say that I am is really a summary of what I have done, or lived through, in the past, such as applying for and being given a job, having carried out its expected duties up till now, and so on. This is not something which really characterizes me as I am now, for it is up to me at this moment to decide what to do now, I cannot simply sit back and see what follows from my nature. So although such things as these are what I may say in truthful answer to questions as to what I am, and in this sense are, indeed, what I am, in a more profound sense I am not these things that I am. What I am, however, is precisely that future self which I am now orientating myself to becoming, such as the author of the book I am now composing. It is in that future self, although it is only a possibility which may never come to pass, that I have my truer being. So I am that which I am not, but am orientating myself towards being. In the end, indeed, I am in the present nothing – nothing except a past which I am no longer and a future which may never come to be.

We are now encountering the most significant of the contrasts Sartre draws between his two basic sorts of being, the in-itself and the for-itself. The in-itself, or any particular thing within it, has a definite nature and is a definite something. What it 'does' at any particular moment is settled by its own nature, such as its precise molecular constitution, and the circumstances it is presently in. (I put 'does' in quotation marks to emphasize that it is not acting in the sense in which a purposive being does.) The plant grows when the environment is propitious as the necessary result of its own nature. On the other hand, the for-itself has no definite nature which determines what it does. All it has is a past. But it is not its past. It is, indeed, separated from its past by its own nothingness, which seems to be a way of saying that its separateness from its past is an internal negation which bites into its present being, so that just as it is conscious of its physical environment by its own conscious distinctness from it, so its consciousness of its past takes the form of a conscious distinctness from it.

It seems to me that there is a certain clash between the Sartrean view that things within the in-itself have definite natures which settle deterministically what they will do in any circumstances, and the view that, until played on by the light provided by the for-itself, the in-itself is a plenitude of being with no definite character or articulation into distinct things. Perhaps the idea is that the in-itself is such that when thus played upon by an appropriate consciousness it develops into things with these definite natures, though I do not think that that is a quite satisfactory resolution of the difficulty.

However that may be, the present contrast is fairly clear, and certainly revealing. Whether Sartre is ultimately right in holding that as an individual consciousness I have no nature which settles what I shall do, and that nothing from outside me settles it either, he is certainly right that what I do is not settled in some direct way by the characterizations I might give of myself in trying to say what I am, and that, none the less, it is a pervasive human habit to attempt to give oneself and others the sense that they are thus settled.

As Sartre sees it, we are all constantly characterizing ourselves to ourselves and to others as individuals with certain personality traits, certain social roles, and perhaps certain moral obligations which we are under, which settle what we are doing here and now. This is because we cannot bear the anguish which comes from the full realization that it is entirely up to my totally free choice what I shall do now, and that I have no nature which will settle this for me. If I lose my temper this is not because I am a person with a bad temper, but represents my free choice to deal with the situation which confronts me here and now by meeting it with a certain kind of emotional paroxysm. This paroxysm does not overpower me, rather I assume it in my freedom. The truth that I am a person with a bad temper, granted it is a truth, is a fact about my past, the fact that I have adopted this stance on many past occasions. Or if it is not simply this, but genuinely concerns my future, it is because I have assumed it as my free project to continue to deal with certain sorts of situation in this way. In the former case being bad-tempered is a case of my not being what I am, in the latter it is a case of my being what I am not.

In making myself think that I am losing my temper (kicking the chair or the cat, speaking vehemently, even having certain inner feelings) because I have a bad temper, which now overpowers me, I deceive myself and am in *bad faith* – the best known concept of Sartrean thought. Bad faith in this kind of example, and many others which Sartre explores at great length and mostly with great subtlety, is a deceiving of oneself. Yet in order to deceive myself I must know that about which I annul knowledge in myself, and this seems a contradiction. Sartre will have nothing to do with any such suggestion as that there are two parts of me, one of which deceives the other. In particular, he rejects the idea that some unconscious part of my mind tricks the conscious part. Such deliberate tricking could only be done by a consciousness, and in self-deception it is the same consciousness that deceives and is deceived. Any theory which bifurcates the individual consciousness into two interacting consciousnesses would falsify the unity of consciousness without being able to give any account of how these two distinct consciousnesses communicate, since evidently they cannot communicate as different persons do by way of observing each other's physical being.

Bad faith replaces the unconscious in the Sartrean view of the human mind. Bad faith is a kind of pretending to oneself that one does or does not have certain intentions, while all the time one is aware of having these intentions without there being any real separation between the failure to know this which one has brought about within oneself and this awareness of it. The possibility of bad faith turns upon the distinction between what Sartre calls the pre-reflective cogito and the reflective cogito. (The expression 'cogito' refers to the self-awareness of consciousness first stressed by Descartes in his presentation of the 'cogito ergo sum' theme.) Consciousness can never harbour anything of which it is not totally conscious. To wish to do something, to be sad, to think and so forth is always at the same time to be conscious of oneself as wishing, being sad, and thinking, or rather it is for consciousness to be conscious of itself as being such, since as we have seen it is really consciousness which is conscious, not something, such as a person, which possesses consciousness as one of its properties. (Ultimately the person is a kind of object which consciousness creates as a persona which figures in the world of which this and other consciousnesses are conscious, a kind of falsely substantialized version of itself which deputizes for it in the in-itself.) This awareness of everything about itself which pertains to consciousness is not, however, properly speaking, knowledge, since this requires some kind of distinction between knower and known such as is absent here. Consciousness is self-illuminating and self-illuminated without having a division within it between knower and known. Yet this division can occur in reflection, when I do in a manner separate into the self which knows itself and the self which knows. Thus in bad faith consciousness in full pre-reflective self-awareness provides itself with a reflective pseudo-knowledge of itself. Otherwise put, it brings itself under concepts which clash with what pre-reflectively and nonconceptually it is aware of itself as being.

Bad faith of one sort or another is the all but constant state of a human being, though it can take forms which differ greatly in the degree of self-deception. There is a deep reason why bad faith is so pervasive, which is that there is something terrible about the truth concerning consciousness in every case, namely that it is, in the way we have considered, a nothingness. The for-itself is a kind of gap in being, a kind of locus hollowed out in the plenitude of being in which there is instead of a something a kind of nothingness, aware of itself as being so and desperate to become a something. The most appalling thing about this nothing is its total freedom as to what it will make itself. For in fact the nothingness of present consciousness does at every instant make itself into something, though as soon as it has done so that something becomes the past of a new nothingness. Thus in everything I do I am really freely choosing to do it, yet I try, in bad faith, to represent myself to myself as doing it because I have a nature which compels me thus to act. Life, therefore, is a constant pretending, a constant playing of roles.

Under the heading of bad faith Sartre includes both fairly straightforward cases of self-deception, adopted in particular situations, and much more long-term ways of living one's life. The woman who leaves her hand in that of a man who has taken it may be tricking herself into thinking that she is not aware of the advance being made to her. For her reflection she is a person so engaged in the conversation that she does not notice anything else, but at the level of pre-reflective consciousness she is aware that she is refraining from restraining the man's approach. The politician who seethes with indignation at some act of his opponents is for reflection an honest man carried away by his feelings, but at the pre-conceptual level he is consciously seeking an opportunity for self-advancement. British politicians who get worked up about some slight or danger to the royal family are, surely, engaged in a long-term political life of bad faith, for this is a kind of concern which can only be synthetic.

One main type of bad faith is exhibited for Sartre by all the dignified people he calls 'serious'. Everyone who really identifies himself with his position in society and does not bring it home to himself that he is engaged in a kind of charade is disguising from himself that he has never really grown into his role but is play-acting it. When we are young adults we order meals at restaurants with self-conscious assurance, but as older adults we may well have a sense that we are still children playing at being grown-ups. If we have this sense in a lively fashion we are admitting to ourselves what more serious individuals have hidden from themselves, that they are still only children at play; moreover, if Sartre is right, even when we were children we were only playing at being such. These last examples are not much in the vein of Sartre himself but are, I believe, true to his thought. He put it nicely in his autobiography, when he said that like all men of his generation, including Victor Hugo, his grandfather was under the impression that he was Victor Hugo, an example, in Hugo's case, of not being what one is.

Bad faith, in general, then, is an attempt by that emptiness or nothingness which is an individual for-itself to pretend to itself that it has the satisfying definiteness of character of a something. We all know, at least from novels, about the actor who falls into mere emptiness when not before an audience. For Sartre we are all actors trying to be an audience towards ourselves. Thinking along these lines, he dismisses as self-deception any apparent being overcome by an emotion. One is not made sad by an event, one decides to greet it with an assumption of sadness.

Is there then no escaping bad faith? Sartre's view seems to be that it is rare, but that to the extent that we are conscious to ourselves of making ourselves what we are at this moment by a free choice we may move beyond it. For reflection may be impure or pure. It is impure when consciousness presents itself to itself in reflective mood as something undergoing certain states of mind which come upon it (such as a surge of love or anger), but it is pure when consciousness notes the freedom with which it is making the decisions it is making.

It is convenient to use the word 'decision' here, but in fact Sartre thinks of decision, understood as a weighing of pros and cons, as just one attitude we may adopt in free spontaneity on the same level of not being something which is truly us as is the being overcome by emotion. When one deliberates one has freely chosen thus to deliberate at a much deeper level of choice, and has probably chosen already the decision with which the deliberation will end so that there tends to be something essentially fraudulent about it. (Talk of a deeper level, here, is misleading, of course, if it suggests something unconscious, as opposed to something not conceptualized and put into words.)

Sartre illuminates many aspects of human life along these lines. Besides, the whole idea that as individual consciousnesses we are a kind of emptiness desperately striving to be a something casts a light on human life which goes beyond what seems to fall under 'bad faith'. Sartre holds that the urge to possess things is an effort to merge oneself in the things one owns, and become thing-like along with them. In the end, on his view, all desire, and thus all action, is directed to becoming something with a definite character. One sees the future beckoning as a time when all this uncertainty as to what one is will be over and one will have discovered one's métier as something to recline in with a sense of settled achievement. Sartre says that the ultimate human aim is to become God. By this he means to become something with an absolute definite nature, unlike this emptiness one finds within oneself, but which is at the same time for-itself, that is, conscious. Yet this goal is incapable of achievement, for only the in-itself, the nonconscious, can have a definite character. Consciousness is capable of being outside itself and being about other things just because it has no inside to escape from.

Sartre has developed one of those deeply pregnant ways of looking at things which one can become so immersed in that one finds almost everything one comes across lends itself to being interpreted in the light of it, and this is evidently because there is a great deal in it. But it hardly does full justice to the human condition. That Sartre has spoken so deeply to people in the twentieth century suggests that it is typical of our age to feel a kind of alienation of oneself from the role one finds oneself playing. His philosophy is, above all, a strong plea for sincerity, sincerity in admitting that one is never deeply involved and at one with what one is doing.* But surely one has many feelings thrust on one which one does not in any way choose to have.

The person who wishes to be cultured goes to art galleries, and it is, I presume, common to look at paintings and decide to oneself what to feel about them. What a relief it is when a real feeling of delight comes over one, and one realizes that there is something other than this drudgery of appreciation. Watching dreadful events on television news, one may set oneself to be shocked. A whole range of emotions which people have in response to current situations is adopted with more or less full consciousness of being so. Yet a sudden feeling of fear at how these events may impinge on oneself, or perhaps a less interested distress at what is going on, may come upon one. And when one hears news that some friend or relation has died, one may start off with a girding oneself to feel the right feelings, only a little later to be struck with a feeling which is in no way assumed. In the latter case one discovers that, contra Sartre, one has a nature, perhaps a rather simple one, that of a doting parent perhaps, without any choice in the matter at any level. Or so at least it seems to me.

The suggestion that the basic motive of human conduct is the search once and for all really to be something with a conclusively settled nature is striking, but surely a fair amount of what lends itself to being thus interpreted can be seen more realistically as a simple search by a being surrounded by threats to its comforts, and perhaps the necessities of its life, to reach a state where these will be finally guaranteed. The search for absolute safety is as much a will of the wisp as is the search of the for-itself for a plenitude of being, but it is more concrete considerations about nature and society which show us that it is so than the rather abstract doctrines about consciousness which show to Sartre that we can never finally be anything. I do think Sartre one of the profoundest of psychologists, but like others he has, perhaps, been so gripped by an insight into a range of situations that he has made it the basis of a theory expressed in terms too universal.

Although the in-itself has a definiteness of character lacking to the for-itself and each part of it acts in a manner determined by its character, it is not a realm which offers any real satisfaction to that quest for rational explanation which is an important aspect of the for-itself's yearning for being. For there is no explanation of why the in-itself is there at all, or why it is there with the particular characters it has. The realm of physical

* Sartre himself uses 'sincere' to refer to a particular life ploy of bad faith – indeed he also often uses 'good faith' thus as well, but I am expressing his thought, as I understand it, in my own terms here.

reality is absurd, '*de trop*', superfluous. When this fact about it really strikes us we may be overcome by nausea. In being so overcome, our attention turns towards the way in which, after all, these definite natures we find there are in the end really only there for us. The reality which lends itself to being described in our conceptual language is not really captured by it. It is just revoltingly there in an opaqueness which offends our own transparency. For, after all, there is one way in which consciousness does have the edge on the in-itself. In its sense of itself as for ever creating itself it does in a sense grasp that it is its own explanation. I do what I do because I have chosen to do it. There is a kind of ultimate explanation of what I am here. It is not an explanation of the fact that I exist as a nothingness which has the task of making itself a something which it no sooner becomes than it is there for it only as its past, but it is a kind of intelligibility all the same. As opposed to this, the in-itself as something there with a certain conceptually ungraspable character has no kind of explanation within itself for its being. The for-itself which becomes sensitive to this truth about the in-itself is nauseated (in a manner described most fully in Sartre's novel, *Nausea*).

This is true of one's own body, and each of us, or so Sartre thinks, is overcome at times by this meaningless object we are involved with, and in a manner feel ourselves to be. We experience what he calls 'the taste' of our own body, while the fleshiness of others is the taste which we know they must experience of themselves as revealed to us. The ultimate unintelligibility of more alien parts of the in-itself is bad enough, but that of our own body is especially upsetting because it is the unintelligible basis of our own (negative type of) being as a consciousness. In these thoughts Sartre shows himself as an eccentric example of the dualist tradition for which the body is a troubling encumbrance, though he differs from traditional dualism in seeing the encumbrance as also our source.

For Sartre one's body is not oneself as consciousness, on the other hand it is the something with which the nothingness of consciousness is most immediately bound up. One's experience of oneself as embodied brings home to oneself the fact that however much one's consciousness has to choose what to be, the fact that it is at all is due to naturalistic circumstances in the in-itself which are sheer matter of fact with no ultimate intelligibility. One's body is also, obviously, the most immediate vehicle of one's agency and gives one one's situation in the world. It is also the basis of one's being there for others as a reality they can know about.

But how can one be sure that there are any others? Sartre devotes much time to the philosophical problem of other minds, the problem of how one can know that one is not the only reality, or at least the only consciousness, in the world. In offering his answer to this problem he develops a certain somewhat chilling view of personal relations.

Philosophers have long concerned themselves with the problem of solipsism, the problem of how I know that I am not all that is. Sartre holds that the certainty I have of my own existence as a consciousness, that captured in the Cartesian 'cogito ergo sum', is inseparable from a certainty that things of which I am conscious exist. We have already seen that he took over from Husserl the idea that intentionality, being of or about something, is the most essential feature of consciousness, and he took this to imply that if there is consciousness there is also some object, other than consciousness, which it is of. The idea is, perhaps, that though one may get all sorts of things wrong in detail, one cannot be wrong in taking it that there is some kind of reality distinct from one's present consciousness on to which it was directed. This swift way with solipsism would surely satisfy few – it would not, indeed, satisfy Husserl – since the fact that one needs to distinguish thinking or perceiving from what is thought of or perceived does not show that the latter really has the independent existence one may be crediting it with. Still, Sartre thinks that the issue of solipsism is to be met by noting how consciousness points beyond itself.

He applies the same kind of thinking to the problem of other minds. Certainly not all consciousness points to itself as being together in the world with other consciousnesses, but there is one kind of consciousness which does so, and which can, therefore, be taken as the basis of a special cogito of other minds – I experience this, therefore there is consciousness other than my own. Sartre thinks this is true of the consciousness of the look, of being looked at by another. This may take various forms, for example shame or fear. I have been doing something in private (Sartre's own example is that of looking through a key-hole, a less than perfect example, since such looking surely always carries with it an awareness of the consciousness of those observed – perhaps some private act of physical relief would serve better), and suddenly I hear a noise which suggests to me that I am observed. I thus become aware of myself as existing as an object of another's awareness, and thus of their awareness as a reality distinct both from my consciousness and the mere objects in the world at which it is directed.

Sartre contends that this sense of being an object of awareness to others is the basic form of our recognition that there are other consciousnesses, and that, although I may be wrong in any particular case in thinking that I am being looked at, or looked at by a particular kind of person, the experience of being looked at guarantees that in general I am available as an object of observation to real others, just as perception, though it may be incorrect in detail, guarantees that there is a perceivable world. For example, if I am a soldier crawling towards a house, which I have to attack and occupy, I experience myself as vulnerable to regard by others who can assault me in my bodily being, and however much I may be mistaken at any moment in thinking that I am seen, the assurance given me by fear that there are others in the world who may see me is infallible.

Such thoughts certainly bring home the impossibility I suspect we all find in taking any kind of solipsism seriously. To try to think of oneself as the only consciousness there is would be to slough off all concern with the impression one may be making in a manner which no amount of philosophical scepticism will bring about. But this may show simply that there are beliefs we cannot rid ourselves of, and not show that they are in some absolute sense incapable of being mistaken. Actually, I myself think that there are experiences of communion with others which are intrinsically infallible, and perhaps the same is true of some experiences of being looked at. What I rather doubt is whether Sartre is right in giving such pride of place to the experience of being looked at, as against experiences of doing things together with.

In insisting on the primacy of the look, Sartre is deliberately departing from the claim of Heidegger that *mitsein*, or being-with, is one of our basic ways of being in the world, settling the fact for us that we are members of a community of conscious individuals before any explicit thinking about the nature of the world we are in arises. For Sartre, a sense of being together with others in some common activity arises only after we are assured by the sense of being looked at by them that there are others. He claims that the real basis of the sense of being-with lies again in the look, the sense of being observed by a third as acting together with someone else. His arguments for the primacy of the look appear to me a little thin, but it is an idea which certainly leads him to a series of intriguing observations about human relationships.

There is something terrible about the experience of the look, for it is of its essence that I recognize myself as being something which I cannot bring home to myself in my own consciousness. The person I am for others, at least if they know me well, is something I have to acknowledge as being myself, yet I do not really know what this person is. Thus I am aware of others as having a hold over me, for they see what I am, as I cannot.

As I am for others I have a definite character, somewhat as the in-itself does, yet they are aware of me as for-itself, and my perceived body is taken in as manifestation of a for-itself made object. It might seem that this gives me what, according to Sartre, is the ultimate goal of every for-itself, a sense of itself as after all being a something rather than a nothingness. Yet it does not provide this in the longed-for form. For one thing, I cannot get hold of this kind of objectified for-itself which I recognize myself as somehow being; it exists only for others, and cannot give me the satisfaction I want. Moreover, in so far as I do get some inkling of it this only produces a despairing sense of its contrast with the nothingness I am for myself.

Sartre is a lover of paradox, and this means that if one ever suspects an incoherence it will probably be one he himself has delighted in developing as a paradox built into the human situation. Realizing that a response of this kind to the objection is implicit in what he says, I still think that it is incoherent to take the look as the basic way of being conscious of others as conscious, since this amounts to saying that one person's consciousness of another's consciousness is primordially consciousness of the latter's consciousness of oneself. But, so to speak, if that is so, how can awareness of each other as conscious beings ever get started? It would be different if the look gave consciousness simply that one is present as a body to the consciousness of others. But this is not the idea, though the example of the soldier's fear may suggest it, since the special place given to shame shows that the look makes one aware of oneself as being present as a for-itself to others. Surely it cannot be satisfactory to explain awareness that another is conscious as the grasp that he grasps one's own consciousness, if the same must be said of this knowledge he has of one's own consciousness, or at least of his first grasp that there are conscious others.

From the Sartrean point of view, in any case, human relations derive their character above all from this fact that their basis lies in the way in which I somehow lose control and understanding of my own being by figuring in the world of others. Or rather I lose hold of my being in the very act of acquiring it, for before I was something for others, and recognized this, I had no sense of myself as being an individual at all – there was simply the presence of the world to a nothingness.

There are two basic ways in which for-itselfs try to deal with this problem. In the first I try to gain a sense of this being which I am for others by a kind of identification with their consciousness in which as possessor of their consciousness I come into possession of myself as I figure there. In the second I try to quell the other's subjectivity by making it something which exists only as an object in the world of which I am aware.

Love and masochism are given as main species of the first attitude to others. The masochist attempts to make himself nothing but an object in the hands of the other, he seeks to bathe in the other's look and be nothing but what is seen there, but at the same time he seeks to control the kind of look, the kind of stance, the other is taking towards him. Thus the uneasy question hovering constantly in our minds as to how the I which I am for myself stands to the I which I am for others is damped down, for I have no subjectivity of my own, but only a participation in that subjectivity of the other in which I am merely object. But, of course, I cannot really get what I want, for I need to control the other's subjectivity for this purpose, and that means that in one way or another a contrast is set up between his real subjectivity and that with which I identify. Love comes under the same heading for Sartre, since love, in particular sexual love, is essentially the wish to be loved, that is to give oneself up to the other's subjectivity as an object totally theirs to do what they want with. Thus both love and masochism are versions of the desire of the nothingness which is a for-itself to be a something, a something observed and handled and commanded as an object by the other.

The main species of the second attitude to the other are sadism, hate and sexual desire. In all these I try to get rid of the other as a free subjectivity in whose look I exist as a kind of object by making him (him or her, of course) into a mere object. I might do this in hate by killing him, though this will prove no real success because his look is directed at me all the more intensely from the past. Or hate can take the form of a kind of positive indifference, in which the other person's subjectivity is simply a kind of process in the world, an attitude which Sartre detects in some psychological theorizing. When I think of another's subjectivity thus, I do not recognize him as casting a look on *me*, but as simply having a kind of psychical occurrent in his stream of consciousness, which we may call an image of me, but which is so separate from me that I need not worry about it.

Sexual desire is another way in which I try to get rid of the other's subjectivity. In this case my concern with the other's body, directed particularly at 'masses of flesh which are very little differentiated ... breasts, buttocks, thighs, stomach' is with the body as consciousness coagulated or ensnared in matter. Lust is not concerned with the other's consciousness as such, but nor is it concerned with the body as sheer inanimate form and quality. It is concerned with the body as the expression or incarnation of consciousness in which it loses as much of its character of freedom as is possible compatibly with its still remaining consciousness. In caressing the other lustfully I try to make them sheer fleshiness both for myself and for themselves and thus annihilate that freedom in which I exist as the object of a look which gives me a character I cannot realize in my own consciousness.

Sadism represents a fiercer way of trying to obliterate another's subjectivity, so that one's own reality does not drain away from that which one grasps of it to the being which it has for the look of another.

Many people feel that though there is much that is illuminating in these Sartrean analyses his whole approach is, as I once heard it well put, 'insufficiently zoological'. Surely the main explanation of lust lies in the devices for keeping the species or genes going developed in the particular kind of animal we are through natural selection, and in side effects of this development, which do not directly serve survival of the species or genes but are bound to what does. However, Sartre thinks that sexuality belongs to something more intrinsic to consciousness than this, not turning on what are contingent facts which might have been otherwise about the physiology and modes of reproduction of the organisms in which consciousness has emerged, but on the need one consciousness has to make an object of another, to escape its look. The physical facts of our make-up channel this ontological necessity into particular modes, but our physical needs are not what give sex the pervasive place it has in human life. Sartre sees similar ontological significance in other physical needs, such as eating, contending that the varying tastes in food of individual persons reflect the different ways in which consciousness seeks to be an in-itself, the different textures reflecting different compromises between freedom and definiteness, so that one person will prefer the more and the other the less solid.

Thus the lack of zoological naturalism in his approach to human nature (to use an expression he repudiates) is pervasive, not limited to his treatment of some particular type of desire. In spite of the total freedom he ascribes to every consciousness, there are certain universal structures which belong to consciousness as such, in particular its hopeless quest to become a something.

It is, surely, a serious objection to this philosophy that there seems no satisfactory account which can be given in terms of it of animals. Does an animal, say a highly developed one such as a rat, dog or cat, belong wholly to the level of the in-itself or does it have a consciousness which is an example of the category of the for-itself? I can see only three replies which a Sartrean might give, and none seems convincing. The first is to hold with Descartes that animals are unconscious automata. The second is to hold that they have a consciousness, but that it does not have that constantly self-creating freedom which is the key feature of the Sartrean for-itself. The third is to hold that, even if in a less intense way, they do, as consciousnesses, answer to the Sartrean account of the for-itself, and that they create their being freely, while remaining ultimately a nothingness distinct from what they make of themselves.

The first reply can hardly be taken seriously. The second allows that there may be a consciousness which has a definite nature which settles what it does, and therefore puts in doubt the basic Sartrean tenet that consciousness and freedom are one, and at least suggests that there may be human conscious behaviour which may be explained in a more deterministic fashion than Sartre allows. As for the third, Sartre himself would be unlikely to endorse it, but I am quite ready to believe that there is a kernel of non-deterministic freedom in animals in any sense in which there is in man. But are animals then sometimes in bad faith, and at other times not? There is something a trifle odd in the idea of rats living a life of bad faith in which they refuse to admit to themselves that they act as they do because they choose thus, not because they have a given nature. It would be only a little less odd to see them as acting in the anguish, at times, of an unevaded freedom. Yet if we say that these categories do not apply to the unreflective freedom of animals, it suggests itself that there may be human consciousnesses too which just get on with their lives, without the question of bad faith, or its surmounting, arising. This is very likely true, but dents the universality of the Sartrean characterization of man.

Thus considerations of our affinities to animals may lead us to doubt whether the Sartrean conception of the for-itself as both free and in agony at being so is altogether satisfactory. And surely the fact that we are moulded in our characters by our social situation, not to mention genetic factors, conflicts with it. How free does Sartre really think we are?

The Sartre of *Being and Nothingness* seems to claim that there is nothing about me which I have not assumed by an act of free choice. That human beings have characters on the basis of which we can form definite expectations with regard to them, and in terms of which we can understand them, rests upon the fact that each for-itself is always engaged upon some project which, taken in conjunction with the particular circumstances holding at any time, does settle, more or less specifically, what it will do at any time. However, this project is something adopted at some stage in the past which is renewed at each moment by a tacit free endorsement, and the possibility always exists for everyone of a total break with the past and adoption of a quite new project. To understand a human being is to understand the basic project in terms of which he is living his life, and for a human being to come to understand himself is for him to bring to a reflective consciousness, which is purer than the ordinary reflection upon ourselves which we conduct in bad faith, the choice of project he has adopted pre-reflectively and to realize that if he goes on living a life informed thereby it is not because either his character or his circumstances dictate this, but because he continues freely to rechoose that project at every moment. We must emphasize again that this fundamental choice of project does not come about as a result of deliberation, since deliberation, and the attaching of a certain weight to certain sorts of consideration, itself stems from a project to be rational in this manner rather than, say, to be one who is carried away by passion. The choice of project is, for Sartre, a kind of deeply spontaneous non-reflective occurrence, and I confess myself to seeing little difference between saying that it just happens, as Sartre would not say, and saying that it is something one does freely, as he insists. (When I discuss Spinozism I shall suggest that a more deterministic version of this Sartrean doctrine is possible.)

The person who complains that his circumstances set limits upon the projects available to him is as self-deceptive, according to the Sartre of the existentialist period, as one who says he is a victim of his character. The statement of this point sometimes takes on an exaggerated form in which it borders, as it seems to me, on absurdity (as Sartre himself came to think later), as when it is said that there are no accidents, and no innocents in war, since each has chosen the situation of these accidents or of this war. (This certainly sounds bizarre and indeed unpleasant, if one thinks of injured babies.) Put more soberly, as it often is, the idea is that there are no brute facts about the situation anyone is ever in, which one can describe in a manner which concerns only what they have to deal with, as opposed to how they are dealing with and conceiving it in terms of their own projects.

In short, if someone has certain problems to deal with these are only problems for him because he has certain projects which run into difficulty, and it is impossible to describe what produces these difficulties in terms which do not reflect the project. The bare facts about the environment as they would be for him whatever his problem belong to an inconceivable world of mere 'in-itself'. Mountaineers in difficulties see the mountain in terms of the extent of their wish to reach the summit, the amount of distress and danger they will go through before deciding to give up, their own skills and methods of climbing and the type of cooperative relation which holds between the members of the team and so forth. There is really nothing which would be the same about the mountain whatever one's projects. For the viewer of scenery, or the photographer or painter, it is something quite different. So-called objective facts about its height, its geological constitution, and its vegetation concern what it becomes when certain procedures of measurement or classification are applied to it, and so forth. Each for-itself makes its own world out of some kind of common raw material, but the raw material is uncharacterizable, and we cannot distinguish what is created out of it by our projects, and what it itself contributes.

For simplicity, I have spoken as though this raw material consisted solely of the context of nonconscious in-itself in which a for-itself finds itself at any moment, but of course it includes in inextricable combination the projects of other for-itselfs with whom I am in relation and the worlds determined by these projects. These worlds interpenetrate with mine, so that my situation is created from the projects of others as well as my own; however, in the last resort I am free to make what I like of the projects of others, as part of the context in which I am living, as I am of the sheer in-itself. Thus in a war situation each person chooses his own war, making out of the realm of sheer ungraspable facts of physical reality and the projects of others as mere process his own particular world, and just as a mountain is only a mountain for one with a system of classifications which reflect a project in which mountains as such can have a place, so is this true of war, which could not occur in the world of one who had no concern with others as human beings but, perhaps, saw the world as so much matter in motion carrying different kinds of danger or comfort for himself. In the light of this we can perhaps give some kind of sense to the Sartrean endorsement of the statement he quotes that there are no innocents in war. We are to think of people as only present in situations that they grasp. The poor baby who suffers sudden pain is no more living within the war situation than is the grasshopper who perishes in the same conflagration.

There is certainly something in this idea that each person creates her own world.* The idea seems to gain somewhat if one takes it as referring also to the way in which one creates situations in one's own image not merely by the way one conceives them but by one's impact, to put it thus, upon the raw facts themselves, in action. Thus each person moving to a new job makes out of her work a particular kind of situation both by the way she looks at it from the start and by the way she selects others whom she can prompt to responses in which she finds her own typical problems. Where one feels Sartre exaggerates is in seeming to deny that there are any real constraints or assistances from the environment. However, his concern is to insist that these have no describable neutral character and we can only think of them in terms which represent what we have made of them. The nearest to a definite outside factor he acknowledges is the world produced by the project of another, or a group of like others, which there is a special difficulty for me in not taking over as my own world too.

Thus my situation as much as what I do about it is the creation of my freely adopted project, and it is one's project which is the key fact about one. This project is always a project to be something definite by which one will escape from the nothingness, the lack of any definite characteristics, which is the nearest to a nature which a for-itself has. All action is directed at possession, making, doing or being, and, in the end, the first three are all ways of trying to make oneself something. For most people their project is a form of bad faith, because they expect really to become something, or make themselves believe that they have already become it, in which the perpetual task of choosing afresh each moment what to make of oneself, and what kind of world to experience oneself as living in, is at an end and they can simply settle down to being what they are and acting accordingly.

There is, however, the difficult possibility of a project of a freedom which does not seek to hide from itself, and accepts, in anguish, that its lot must be to adopt a role which nothing forces upon it, and to act this out as long as it chooses freely not to rescind it.

There is no objective system of values according to which thus to live in unevaded freedom is what one ought to attempt. The holding of certain moral obligations or values is something which only exists in a world a free for-itself chooses for itself. To think one is acting as one

* I do not know how to use 'he or she' without unbearable clumsiness, hence this brief shift to 'she . I think we must one day turn to a use of 'they' with a singular sense, as I did some pages ago, or it must be accepted that each sex uses the pronoun applicable to – themselves.

does in obedience to a moral law one did not make for oneself is as much bad faith as thinking one is acting in that way because it follows from one's character. Still, in the light of the grasp of the total freedom of the for-itself which she has, the Sartrean existentialist does set out to live in a freedom which is honest with itself.

This project of unevaded freedom, as we might call it, seems to have a double aspect in one of which it points to a rather playful approach to things, in the other of which it points to an existence of tough heroism. It has a playful aspect in which it contrasts with the life of the *serious* person, for whom we have seen that Sartre expresses a particular hostility. The serious person is the respectable member of society who has a certain position which, taken together with moral standards, which he thinks of as just there, settle how he is bound to behave without any acceptable option. The indignant judge who does not see his robes as those assumed in a costume drama, and who finds it his painful duty to sentence the convicted to some grim punishment, however much it goes against his feelings of compassion, is a paradigm case of such seriousness. As against this, the for-itself living in unevaded freedom, should it play such a role, which is perhaps unlikely, will realize that the indignation, together with the moral standards which support it, are things it has freely introduced into its world, and well up in him or hover over him of his own choice. The life of unevaded freedom will, then, it would seem, have a certain lightness of touch in its approach to things.

Yet if we contrast this life of unevaded freedom not so much with the grimness of seriousness as with its contented complacency, it will stand out as likely to face us with truly heroic demands. Many people who live comfortable lives are aware that they are surrounded by sufferings stemming from the social organization of which they are the beneficiary, but they think of society as an inevitable structure, for the character of which they are not responsible, which provides them with a definite niche which it is simply in the nature of things that they should fill just as they do. In their relations with their family, work associates and others they simply do what they ought to do and are not to blame for the fact that the world is not perfect. As against this, the truly honest for-itself will realize that if he lives in a world in which for such a person thus to live in comfort is just the thing to do, and in which, say, there is not even the question of engaging in radical and dangerous underground political activity, that is his choice, and he must then contemplate the wretchedness surrounding him as something he has personally chosen as something to be accepted. The world in which one exists wears the image of oneself, and if one cannot (or rather will not) frankly face that image as one's own creation, as probably one cannot (or will not), a much more painful life is indicated as one's thereby freely adopted lot. Existentialism points to heroism by insisting that there is no ducking one's complete personal responsibility for any state of affairs one takes as tolerable.

It is difficult not to feel that there is a kind of ethical objectivism lurking in this heroic side of existentialism, an assumption that there are certain things which it is only through evasions that anyone takes as tolerable. Sartre's own personal sense of the iniquities of the existing state of human affairs, always strong, intensified during the war years, and, canalized into more definite political commitments as he watched the behaviour of the dominant governments and classes of the world to the third world, and all the oppressed, in the years after the war. led him to ever more active identification with extreme left Marxist causes. Philosophically, also, he moved much closer to Marxism, and came to see a highly qualified existentialism as serving mainly to preserve a sense of human freedom within the content of Marxist thinking. He came to acknowledge that the claims concerning total freedom he had advocated ignored the extent to which it was limited by social and economic circumstance. However, he continued to insist that, whatever the constraints might be, each individual consciousness has a real latitude as to what it makes of, and does in the context of, its situation at every moment.

I have made no attempt to explore the thought of this later more Marxist Sartre. His earlier existentialist philosophy remains a particularly distinctive 'theory of existence' worthy of exploration in its own right.

[EIGHT]

SPINOZISTIC PANTHEISM

We come now to a 'theory of existence' adherents of which are likely to claim that it does justice to the element of truth in each of the other theories, although it is by no means a mere patchwork of different theories sewn together, but a highly unified doctrine in its own right. In its original form, as presented by Spinoza (1632–77) in his *Ethics*, first published shortly after his death in 1677, it could hardly indeed have been intended as a synthesis of such doctrines as are presented here, since many of them were only developed long after his death. Still, he did, it would seem, to some extent see it as a kind of synthesis of various doctrines which were familiar in his day, and in fact he produced a comprehensive view of the world into which the insights of many later philosophers can be introduced as further developments of some of its details.

Spinoza was a Jew of Portuguese descent who lived in the Netherlands. He was excommunicated from his synagogue in his youth for his heterodox opinions, and he lived thereafter a somewhat retired life as a grinder of optical lenses, but in contact with, and much respected by, some of the most distinguished thinkers and statesmen of his day. What has appealed mainly to the many people ever since who have been deeply influenced by his thought is usually not so much the details of his argumentation but his general vision of the nature of reality, and of man's true good. In what follows I shall sketch a view of the world which is essentially Spinozistic, but in which the argumentation and some of the details of doctrine are rather what I think is best said today by one who would recommend a Spinozistic point of view on things than summaries of just what he said himself. I have been largely adopting that approach with the other thinkers too, but shall do so even more in this case. That is partly because much of Spinoza's own presentation is in terms of concepts it would take us too far away from our main purposes to attempt to

153

explicate with any fullness. I should emphasize that Spinoza is to a quite unusual extent a thinker who has been understood in different ways by different interpreters, partly because of his famously elliptical presentation, in the form of an axiomatic system (with axioms, definitions and theorems) akin to that of Euclid, partly because of the many different aspects of his thought on which they put different emphases. So what follows is the picture of the world and of the part man does best to play in it to which I move myself when the spirit of Spinoza comes over me.

For the Spinozist Nature itself, or the universe as a whole, is God. Spinozism is thus a form of pantheism, this being the doctrine that God and the whole of things are one and the same.

Were this thesis no more than the decision to use the word 'God' to denote the totality of all that is, it would be at best vacuous, at worst an excuse to go on speaking of there being a God, when his existence in any ordinary sense is denied. There have always been charges that Spinoza was really an atheist who, from a residual piety, liked to be able to use quasi-religious language in talking about the universe. However, there is much more to his position than is recognized by those who make this charge. For he calls Nature or the Universe 'God', because he thinks that it answers to certain descriptions usually thought of in the developed Judaeo-Christian tradition as specifying some of the most important traits which make God God.

One of the things which make God God, according to this tradition, is that He exists necessarily. Whereas every ordinary thing is such that it might well not have existed, for all at least we can see when we consider it in comparative isolation, in the case of God it would have been impossible that He should not have existed. For one who grasps sufficient of what God is, the idea that He might not have existed is as ridiculous as is the idea that there might have been a triangle with four angles. We saw this idea at work in the ontological argument of Descartes in the first chapter. According to this argument we can recognize that God exists by recognizing what kind of being it is concerning whose existence or not we are wondering; when we reflect upon this kind of being, or essence, we realize that it simply had to be actualized in a really existing being.

One weakness of the ontological argument is that it specifies what the essence of God is in such a way that the supposed insight that this essence has to be actualized looks suspiciously like a piece of verbal legerdemain. However, even those who reject the ontological argument, but who believe in the existence of God on one basis or another, usually agree that God is such that if one did adequately know his nature, as He himself must, then one would see that somehow that nature had to be actualized in reality. They agree, that is, that, while however fully one knew the nature of this table in front of me, or even the nature of my very self, one would not see its or one's own existence as a fact to which there was never any alternative, in the case of God the matter must be different. Whether or not, as proponents of the ontological argument believe, one, as a human being, has *the insight into the nature* of God which would reveal why it would have been impossible for him not to exist, it is usually agreed that any being who can properly be called God must be unique in *having such a nature*. For the alternative bids one think that God just finds himself existing, as we find ourselves existing, without there being any reason for his being there. In our case we can, indeed, find an explanation of why we exist in things outside us, such as in the coupling of our parents, or, from a rather different point of view, in the creation of us by God, but in the case of God it is clear that He cannot find a reason why He exists in something outside himself, so that either there must be something about his very nature which explains why He does and had to exist, or his existence is just a kind of inexplicable fluke, something which would rob him of the role of the ultimate explanation of things which it seems He must play in order to deserve his title.

The Spinozist entirely accepts all this, but he thinks that it points to a conception of God in some respects different from usual. It shows for one thing that God and space are the very same thing, for if one casts around for an example of something which could not have failed to exist it seems that space certainly fills the bill. One can imagine anything one likes absent from space, as the philosopher Kant said later, but one cannot imagine space itself absent. Actually the Spinozist does not think of God as empty space, since he identifies space with the total spatially extended universe. What is called a vacuum is just a state one part of space can be in for a time, while containing an object with certain qualities is just another kind of state that space can be in with respect to a certain part of itself. Thus what we really cannot think away is some kind of universe spread out spatially, and so this spatial universe, in that it could not fail to exist, is possessed of one of the main properties which we think of as making God God.

This would hardly justify calling the spatial universe as a whole God, if that were all. But in fact there is another reality which one cannot really think of as something which might never have existed. This reality is *thought* or, as it may be better to call what the Spinozist really has in mind, consciousness. It is not your consciousness or mine which is in question here, but consciousness in general. One cannot really make sense of a world in which consciousness is absent. To think of any state of affairs is to think of it as presented to some consciousness, and to think of the total universe as existing as a totality is to think of it as present as a whole to some total consciousness. If one tries to think of nothing whatever existing, one really thinks of a kind of consciousness existing which is aware of the absence of everything nameable. One can no more think away consciousness than one can think away space, and the space, or total spatial world, which cannot be thought away, cannot be thought of as existing without its being exhibited to some consciousness. Nor can one think of it as exhibiting itself to a whole lot of distinct consciousnesses, with no consciousness of the whole of it since in that case the way one of these bits of it was related to another, and for that matter the way the distinct consciousnesses are related each to each, would exist without being exhibited to any consciousness – and the totality would not really exist as a totality, or not be exhibited to any consciousness as such, which, if this line of thought is correct, would come to the same.

Does time exist with similar necessity? Some kind of eternal duration seems, for Spinoza, more a matter of what necessary existence is than something which possesses it. His philosophy could well embrace the Bradleyan view that ultimately there is but one great eternal now. Something of the sort is, indeed, suggested by his problematic discussion of immortality.

We cannot go into Spinoza's arguments on these points further, nor consider what difference it makes that science presents a different notion of the basic nature of the physical world from that which Spinoza employed. The basic thesis is that the more we consider it, the more we will realize that the idea that there might not have been a system of things spread out in some kind of space, and making up a total, even an infinite, unity is really absurd, and that it is also absurd to think that this system could have existed without being exhibited to a cosmic consciousness. The next step, in the establishment of Spinozism, is to show that the consciousness to which the physical world is displayed is not really a different reality from it, but another aspect of the same reality.

In defending a Spinozistic view of the world on my own account, I would argue that the physical characteristics of things comprise either the way one part of the world appears to another part, or, in a more fundamental sense of 'physical', the structural aspect of things, and that what has structure must have something more to it than structure, and that this more can only be conceived as its own inner feeling of its own being. I would contend also that, granted the world is a genuine totality. there must be a kind of unified inner feeling of its own being as such a totality. In talking of the structure of a thing I mean what, if the thing were a piece of music, would be captured of it in a musical score as studied by someone who was deaf, but took in all the formal properties of the reality the score depicts.

That is not quite Spinoza's argument. In effect he contends that there could not be two infinite and necessary beings, because they would condition each other in a way which would rob them of these properties, which is absurd, so that what we grasp as the infinity and necessity of space and what we grasp as the infinity and necessity of a cosmic consciousness is really the grasp of one and the same thing conceived in different ways. Moreover, he thinks, it is very likely that other minds, with a different nature from ours, may grasp the character of the universe in quite other ways which exhibit different aspects of its necessity and infinity. We may note, in passing, that by infinity is meant here more the not being in any way bound or conditioned by anything else than simply endlessness.

If the universe is an infinite consciousness of itself as a whole and in every detail, and is such that it could not have failed to exist, and if it is the only being of which this is true, it certainly seems to be close enough to what is usually understood by God to be thus called. Yet this concept of God diverges from, for example, orthodox Christian ones, in that it thinks that God exists bodily, as the whole physical universe. Yet a physical universe which is conscious of itself through and through is so different from so much mere matter, as we usually think of it, that this conception rather raises our conception of matter than lowers our conception of God. Wordsworth, inspired by his own experiences, was conscious that he was expressing a Spinozistic view of nature when he spoke

> Of something far more deeply interfused,
> Whose dwelling is the light of setting suns,
> And the round ocean and the living air,
> And the blue sky, and in the mind of man:
> A motion and a spirit, that impels
> All thinking things, all objects of all thought,
> And rolls through all things.

This passage from Wordsworth suggests a positive answer to the next question I think one should ask oneself in considering whether it was proper for Spinoza to use the word 'God' to denote nature or the universe, as he conceived it, namely the question whether God or Nature (*Deus sive Natura*, as Spinoza himself said in the Latin in which his main work was written) is a possible object of religious emotion, even of some kind of worship. For it would be unsuitable to call anything 'God' which does not call forth this sort of emotion in those who thus call it. Spinoza himself does not write in very romantic language, but it seems that he felt a kind of cosmic religious emotion towards the self-conscious totality of things in which he believed. We are not called upon to agree with, or feel with, Spinoza in order to grant that if the universe is as he thought, and if religious emotion to it is appropriate, as he thought it was, then the universe is properly called 'God'.

What people tend to feel is missing in Spinoza's God is love for men and goodness. So far as the latter goes, the Spinozist thinks that 'good' and 'evil' are appropriate terms for human beings to use for particular things which are serviceable or harmful to them, but that it is simply ludicrous to call the whole of things good, more particularly if this means 'morally good', though it would be still more ludicrous to call it evil. Here he is somewhat at one with aspects of Hindu feeling which find something to reverence in the terrifying side of nature, as well as in its benign side. On the question of 'love' we may note that Spinoza claimed that 'He who loves God cannot strive that God should love him in return', but also claimed that God loved himself and that man's love of God is part of the love with which God loves himself. Goethe, who regarded himself as a kind of Spinozist, saw in the first of these propositions the expression of a sublime altruism. One cannot give a full but brief account of the meanings with which, set in the context of his work as a whole, these sayings of Spinoza are impregnated, but the general line of his thought is that God delights in the activity through which he develops the world process and in the process as object of that activity, and that in so far as man becomes an active rather than a passive participant in that process he is literally an element in that joy, since human creativity is a part of divine creativity. God, indeed, loves man as an element in the process, but man is simply one important element in the whole, not its uniquely special goal.

In talking of God as creator of the world process I am not forgetting that for Spinoza God is that very process. Spinoza distinguishes between two aspects of God or Nature, *Natura naturans* and *Natura naturata*, Nature 'naturing' (or creating) and Nature 'natured' (or created). God is in continual process of creating himself, the making and the made are united as aspects of his self-conscious being. Since there is nothing outside to frustrate him, his creative activity is pure uninhibited joy.

This is all very fine and large, so the reader may feel, but what light does it really throw on the human situation, and on what we should do about it?

The first thing to note is that for the Spinozist man is simply one particular part of God or Nature. Spinoza, of course, wrote long before the theory of evolution had been developed (except as an occasional stray speculation) and, though he never directly discusses the question of man's origin, he probably believed that, at least during this earth's history, the main different types of thing, including animal species with man among them, had simply always been there and always would be. However, the view that man is a highly evolved animal which has come upon the scene as a result of physically explicable processes, and which is, in principle, intelligible as a purely natural phenomenon, suits well with Spinozism.

As a part of 'God or Nature' the human organism is a part of it, in its spatially extended aspect, while the human mind is a part of it as an infinite consciousness to which that physical totality which is its extended aspect is exhibited. More specifically, the human mind is the consciousness of the human body. To make much sense of this one must take it, I think, that what is really meant is that the human mind is a consciousness of certain processes in the human body, above all, or perhaps exclusively, in the human brain, which produce what we normally call its voluntary behaviour, including speech, or which, via the sense organs, monitor the environment in a manner which guides this behaviour towards what promotes survival of the human form.

It is a peculiarity of Spinoza's precise account of the mind–body relationship that it suggests that human consciousness should consist in a kind of total awareness of what is going on within the body. For he says that the human mind is simply the 'idea' of the human body, which for him means that it is that part of God or Nature, considered as consciousness, which corresponds to that part of it, considered as the physical world, which is known as one's body. That seems to imply that the contents of the human mind must have a one to one correspondence with the parts of the human body, and be arranged in relation to each other in corresponding ways. Yet it is obvious that in actual fact one's consciousness is not such a total awareness of one's body (nor of one's brain if, as seems reasonable, we take it that it is really just this that is in question). Spinoza would probably say that our consciousness would reveal exactly what was going on in our brain to one who saw it in a wider context, but it is doubtful if this resolves the difficulty. It can only be met, I think, if it is said that our mind is the mental version, not of the brain as a whole, but of some especially significant aspect of what is going on in it.

However this may be, the main thing is that, for the Spinozist, there is a wholly physical explanation of every human performance on its physical side, and a wholly mental explanation of that same performance as registered in the agent's consciousness. Both the physical and the mental explanation would refer to processes in non-human nature. However, the processes of so-called inanimate nature are only readily known to us on their physical side, so that they figure for us only as physical explanations. In contrast, our own thoughts are not well known on their physical side and are brought into our explanations rather on their mental or psychological side. Thus in practice we often have to mix physical and psychological explanation, appealing to that aspect of a process which is best known to us. For example, we may explain the stimuli reaching our sense organs physically, and our reaction to them psychologically.

The general pattern of explanation of what goes on in the world, according to Spinoza, lies in the fact that it consists in innumerable individuals, on different levels of complexity and each comprised in a larger one (until the largest of all, nature as a whole, is reached), each of which has a certain nature or essence and a set of inbuilt responses to whatever acts on it from without, which have a tendency to preserve its continued existence with that nature in an environment thus acting on it. On the physical side this is a matter of each thing having some tendency to preserve its physical structure, on the mental side this is a matter of each node of consciousness having a tendency to preserve itself as a particular way of being conscious of a certain physical structure. Thus whenever any individual in the world, whether an atom, a plant, or a human being, does anything there are two factors explaining this, first, its own self-preserving tendency, second, the external stimuli or situation which evoke this particular act of self-preservation. However, the contribution of each factor is in different proportions in different cases, inasmuch as what it does sometimes reveals more about the stimuli which have acted on the thing, sometimes more about the distinctive nature of the thing. Thus, for example, falling towards the earth when released from a height reveals little distinctive about the nature of the falling object, whereas the sprouting of a seed into a certain plant reveals something very distinctive about it; stones in similar soil do no such thing whatever.

Perhaps the former case, that of an object falling to the earth, is not an act of self-preservation at all. If so, this helps rather than hinders Spinoza's case, which rests on the possibility of being able to distinguish that which is effected by an individual physical thing, and in doing which it is active, from what merely happens to it, while regarding both these as equally necessary. It is extremely hard to clarify this distinction, or to be certain how far in the last resort such a distinction is valid as something more than a human way of looking at a situation, and I shall not attempt to plumb the matter further. I shall simply assume that Spinoza is right in thinking that in explaining a change in which some individual is involved, one can distinguish its own individual contribution to the change from that which it suffers passively through the agency of other things, and that all sorts of different proportions between these two are possible. It is a further point of Spinozistic doctrine that in so far as it is a thing's own contribution that explains the change, this is a matter of its acting in a manner which tends to preserve the thing in its own distinctive character. Here again it is both difficult to know how clear Spinoza's own essential concepts are, and how far they actually stand up as applicable to nature as science now suggests it should be understood, though I am inclined to think that enough of what Spinoza has in mind would stand up to scrutiny in these respects to support his essential purposes.

Of these the most important is to underpin a doctrine of freedom, according to which an individual is free to the extent that changes in which it is involved arise from its nisus to preserve itself in its own distinctive character. Such freedom is in no kind of conflict with necessity or determinism, since what a thing will do in any particular circumstance in order to preserve its distinctive nature follows necessarily from that nature.

The ideally free being would be one such that the changes it passes through follow on each other in a manner such that one would need appeal to nothing not included in the thing itself in order to explain them. Such is true of the changes which God or Nature as a whole passes through, and is true in no other case. However, in so far as a human being is thinking rationally the changes in his consciousness to some extent approximate to this. He has set himself, say, a certain mathematical problem, and his thinking passes through a series of stages, till he reaches his conclusion, the main explanation of which lies in the nature of the problem, and the relations between the essences or the concepts which figure in the problem, all of which are actually somehow there within his consciousness. One cannot say that the progress of his thought turns on nothing but that thought's own elements, because his thought might pass to other things at any moment if the environment impinged on him too obtrusively, and an act of violence from the outside world could bring him and his thought to an end at any moment. Still, granted a phase of stability in his environment (under which, indeed, we really need to include bodily processes within the person which are not aspects of his present distinctively human project), the development of his thought is internally determined, and he is, in Spinozistic terms, free, although, or rather because, each stage of his thought follows necessarily on the previous.

Spinoza treats a certain kind of rationality as the distinctive essence of man, a view which may seem narrow, but which fits in neatly with his notion of freedom as internal determination, because, as our example suggests, the project of working out a rational solution to a problem seems capable of setting a series of changes in tow, which are intelligible as its necessary development. We may add that the project to think of that problem rationally can be thought of as the particular version of human rationality which has arisen in that person's history as a result of stimuli from outside. The essential Spinozistic message is that anything can be thought about rationally, so that anything can be grist to the mill of that freedom which is one with rationality; in so far as it becomes food for rational reflection our response to it is active and free. This applies also to our external behaviour: in so far as this is the expression of our understanding of our situation it is free, whether it is behaviour directly orientated in the service of intellectual tasks or whether it is simply a dealing with the environment in our daily affairs which reflects an understanding of our situation and ourselves.

Many who are enticed by Spinoza's picture of freedom, as consisting in thought and behaviour which express one's own nature, would not endorse the highly intellectualistic idea he seems to have of that nature. It may be that this complaint stems from understanding his statements in a narrower sense than they had for him. It is possible, in any case, to enrich the Spinozistic notion of freedom by recognizing types of inner mental necessity which are less intellectualistic. Is it not the case that an aesthetic project lays down a process of thought, or of thought-informed activity, which unfolds with an inner necessity of a less formal kind than that involved in thinking about mathematics? As a novelist works out his story, a composer his symphony, and as a sculptor chips at his stone, is not something unfolding which is necessitated by the project in consciousness from the start combined with the essential nature of the concepts and mentally grasped nature of the raw materials in which the artist is working? Of course, one could not know that their necessary upshot was this work of art until the process was completed, but that was equally true of the solution to the mathematical problem, and does not mean that they were not intrinsically determined by these factors, perhaps combined with more accidental factors which intervened, but got caught up in the unfolding of the project inasmuch as the use to which they were put was determined by this. And having recognized that this may be true of aesthetic creation, should we not recognize it as equally true of any kind of constructive human activity?

Thus we may separate two claims which Spinoza runs together, namely that, in the first place, freedom consists in activity which follows of necessity from an aspect of one's nature which is present in and is grasped within one's consciousness as that engages with whatever affects one's consciousness from outside, and that, in the second place, such activity consists in rational thought. Our suggestion is that, unless rational thought be understood in a very stretched sense, we need not accept the rather narrow conception of human good suggested by the second claim, simply because we accept the first. Such a revised Spinozism seems to do better justice to the variety of human forms of fulfilment inasmuch as the types of human consciousness with a nature capable of such unfolding need not be thought of as all simply different instances of some kind of standard essence known as rationality.

Spinoza's insistence, even if qualified in the way I have been suggesting, on the importance of rationality sorts, in any case, a little oddly with his view that man is to be understood as a part of nature, for if all genuine individuals in nature, such as atoms, plants and animals, have some nisus to preserve their being, and if this exists also as some kind of mental purpose, then we must surely think of this as having some kind of analogy with the creativity of our own consciousness, and the more we think of this in solely intellectualistic terms, the harder this is to credit. Presumably Spinoza must think that, as a seed develops into a plant, by a causal process in which the nature of the plant is active, that portion of the divine consciousness which relates to the specifically plant-like nature of the plant must unfold with a certain degree of that conscious inner necessity which pertains to our minds when they are active. The difficulty seems rather less if we think of rational thought as just one case of consciousness unfolding according to a principle or project somehow lying within it, for we can think of any part of nature which is active to any extent as having a consciousness pertaining to it which at least dimly responds to what intrudes on it from outside so as to sustain or perhaps develop the project of being a consciousness of a sort it feels itself as being. Doubtless it sounds pretty odd to most people to think of nature as ultimately composed of beings which in this sense are at least dimly purposive, but this is a point on which the Spinozist agrees with Schopenhauer and Nietzsche and against any view for which consciousness is the prerogative of humans or even animals. (Spinoza, I should note in passing, attacked vehemently the view that things in nature are there for a purpose, insisting that they simply arise of necessity from the nature of God, not because God is aiming at something beyond them. But this is not meant to be the denial that things have their own individual nisus, reflected in consciousness as a kind of striving after something.)

The Spinozist, then, believes that in the only possible sense in which a man can be free, he is free to the extent that what he does follows from his own consciously grasped nature, and that such freedom, the only freedom which anyone can intelligently want, is compatible with, indeed only intelligible as a form of, necessity. Such freedom is for the Spinozist the supreme value.

If we ask why it is the supreme value, the Spinozist answer is that since the free man is the man who is achieving what he wants, everything that one wants can in the end be subsumed under the end of freedom. Desire, that which lies beneath all behaviour, considered from the mental point of view, simply is the distinctive essence of the agent producing the behaviour necessary to preserve his distinctive nature in the given circumstances, so that in a sense all desire is for self-preservation. The self one wants to preserve is not, of course, some mere piece of living matter in the human form, but a distinctive way of being. I have used the term 'project' to denote the personal way of being one is concerned to preserve, as also the more specific ways of being which, in specific circumstances and in response to specific stimuli, that general way of being develops into. I use the term partly to encourage comparisons with the existentialist philosophy of Sartre. Spinoza is one with Sartre in the central place given to freedom in his thought, but utterly in contrast with him in seeing freedom as the self-actualization of an essence which is simply given, and in no wise chosen (since there is nothing beyond the essence to do the choosing). However, their positions coincide much more than one might expect.

As I understand him, Spinoza sees this freedom which is the ultimate value as one with creativity. However, some would attack the Spinozistic type of creativity, which is determination by factors fully present in consciousness, as a superficial kind of creativity, holding that the really creative consciousness is simply the vehicle for deep forces in the unconscious, or coming perhaps from somewhere right outside the individual mind, with which it is in a contact lost to superficial minds. Stravinsky, speaking in a manner surprisingly reminiscent of that romanticism of which he is supposed to have been the opponent, said that he was simply the vehicle through which the *Sacre* entered the world.

This may be a limitation in Spinoza's outlook. Although he has often been described as a precursor of Freud, it seems that by the mind he essentially means the conscious mind. That is not to say that he does not take account of a good deal of what we might today call the unconscious, but that he regards it as something acting on the mind from outside. Of course, in stressing the importance of being controlled by what lies within, rather than beyond, consciousness, his actual ideal is much what Freud expressed by saying that where *id* was let *ego* be, terms which though not synonymous with *unconscious* and *conscious* function in that saying to express a highly Spinozistic thought.

The contrast between those who see man's good as lying in identification of himself with consciousness and rationality and those who urge the need to be in fruitful contact with perhaps darker aspects of reality is an old one. The views that D. H. Lawrence and Bertrand Russell took of each other are a twentieth-century manifestation of this antithesis. Euripides, in his *Hippolytus* and *Bacchae*, exhibited the dangers run by him who engages solely with the conscious rational aspects of his nature. Perhaps the answer is that there are dark forces within us with which we must find a *modus vivendi*, and that sometimes these give birth to wonders of beauty beyond what is available to the classical projections of the conscious mind, but that it is still the conscious mind which ideally should be in control and decide when to draw upon, and when rather to negotiate more gingerly with, the darker sides of the unconscious.

We have seen that Spinoza was a rigorous determinist, and this is so fundamental to his thought that we must regard determinism as a factor in any outlook which can be called Spinozistic, with perhaps one qualification. Modern quantum physics is usually interpreted as pointing to a level of physical reality at which only statistical laws hold, rather than absolutely deterministic ones. In spite of occasional claims to the contrary, it seems evident that, so far as the more general human implications go, it makes little difference whether what happens throughout nature falls under absolutely deterministic laws, or whether a certain leeway is left to some kind of mere randomness, where physical randomness is not thought of as leaving leeway for some non-physical factor to operate. In short, so far as general *Weltanschauung* goes, a deterministic universe, and one in which determinism is modified by an element of sheer pointless randomness, come to much the same. So I do not think Spinozism as a general outlook is threatened much by these developments in physics, and, for convenience, in talking of determinism in what follows I shall take it that this does not exclude an element of sheer randomness in things. What it does exclude is some other kind of factor, such as might suitably be called *free will*, entering into the explanation of human or any other phenomena. Perhaps the existence of randomness does threaten a certain conception of the universe as totally rational, which is an element in Spinozism, but it does not, of itself, threaten the kind of moral implications Spinoza drew from his determinism. Let us now consider what these implications are.

The Spinozist utterly rejects the idea that anyone is ever to blame for anything undesirable that he has done. A person's actions follow with absolute necessity from his nature in interaction with his circumstances, and it is as pointless to blame him for the fact that he acted as he did, as to blame a triangle for answering to the theorems which follow from its basic definition, or a plant for growing or not growing according to the character of the soil in which it is planted, along with other factors. To blame someone is to feel emotionally about his conduct in a manner which cannot be sustained when you see that conduct as following of necessity from his situation and nature. Even when we do not have such specific insight we can still recognize that there must be an explanation of his conduct, even if hidden from us, such that in the light of the facts the explanation would appeal to, his conduct would be seen as inevitable and as something to which the emotional response of blame would be inept.

What the Spinozist rejects is the emotional aspect of blame. He will not deny that getting annoyed with people, expressing displeasure at their conduct, is sometimes necessary as a way of influencing irrational people to behave better. So far as a person is rational, however, it is more desirable to attempt to show him that in so acting he was either being overpowered by impulses which do not stem from anything which, when brought to clear consciousness, he can really accept as himself, or rested upon some kind of misunderstanding. There is certainly a place for rational expostulation, but it does not take the form of blame, but of bringing someone to see that his conduct is not such as he will want further to engage in when he understands better the true nature of the case. Not that the Spinozist thinks that this kind of rational insight guarantees improvement, since the rational consciousness which he sees as a man's essence is always at risk of being overcome by irrational impulses imposed from outside.

Personal remorse is as irrational as blame of others. Looking back, one should realize that one's conduct was bound to be as it was. Yet as one looks back, and perhaps comes better to understand the state of mind which bred the conduct, one may gain an understanding which will act as a check on similar conduct in future. This will happen if one sees that it arose from only a confused understanding of what solicited one to act thus and its relation to the projects which constitute one's very being. If, the more one understands it retrospectively, the less one is inclined to see such confusion in it, then, in calling it wrong, and feeling remorse, one is simply victim of some conventional categorization of the act as wrong which does not spring from the system of values really appropriate to one whose projects are of that kind. The key to the Spinozist's attitude here is that he identifies himself with his conscious rationality and will not accept that anything to which, in his lucid moments, he objects, really sprang from him.

This way of dealing with emotions of self-blame will seem to many a kind of dodge, indeed a form of bad faith, in which one tries to shuffle away from identification with the past self which chose to act in conscious wickedness. However, the Spinozist might say that, if there is a question of bad faith here, it lies in not being prepared to identify enough with those past choices, which really do spring from that essence which one still is, to see them as right in terms of the project which is oneself, however bad they may be from some conventional point of view which one has not the courage to despise.

It may still seem to the objector to Spinozism that it attempts to deny that in the last resort we act by a choosing which cannot be reduced to a kind of automatic actualizing of our self-preserving and self-developing essence so far as it is not checked by contrary impulses. Even if there is a course of action which is indicated as the rational one, it is not one's rational understanding which produces action along these lines, but a decision to expose oneself to reason rather than to impulse.

This is a forceful objection, yet the proponents of the doctrine of freedom on which it rests have never succeeded in explaining how freedom as a factor in action is other than mere randomness, far as such randomness is from what they wish to speak of. It has been said, in connection with this apparently everlasting dispute, that one should be a determinist about others and a free-will-ist, or libertarian, about oneself. Taken at face value this is scarcely acceptable. However, if it means that there are two different attitudes to action, that of the onlooker, and that of the agent, and that even if the onlooker is right in thinking that action is absolutely determined (or that any indetermination is mere randomness) the agent cannot look upon it thus, and should not pretend to do so, but must be engaged in his decision-making in a manner which does not treat the conclusion as foregone, then I believe it to be along the right lines. This fits in well with a Spinozist attitude to others and to one's past self, and even in the thick of action one need not look upon the conclusion as open, so far as the rational self one is setting out to be, goes, except in the sense in which the one correct solution to a mathematical problem is open till one has found it.

I have hinted above that for the Spinozist the only values to which there can be rational allegiance are those which are recognized as means to, or as elements in, that preserving and enhancing of one's own characteristic type of being which is the sense of all genuinely free activity. Does that imply that a sadist would be foolish to see anything in the morality which bids him check his impulses in acknowledgement of the rights of others? If not, are we in the presence of an immoralism akin to that of Nietzsche?

There are two elements in a Spinozistic answer to this question. Spinoza himself makes it quite clear that a man who clearly saw that the most effective way of preserving his own essence was to commit something others would regard as a crime or a folly would be irrational in not committing it; indeed, if he did not commit it that could only be because forces from outside his own true being dominated him. Although Spinoza sometimes talks as though the sole goal of rational pursuit was self-preservation, it is evident that the self to be preserved is a pattern of thinking and living rather than the preservation of the mere organism, and that in extreme cases survival of the mere organism may have to take second place, as when one sacrifices one's life in order to remain the person one aspires to be. As I have understood, and somewhat developed, Spinozism, this self which one seeks to preserve is really a kind of personal project definitive to oneself of oneself, and one's concern is not simply to preserve but also to enhance it. It seems then that if it were really true that some sadistic individual could only preserve and enhance his particular mode of being by cruelty to others, there is no reason which one could honestly propose to him as a good one why he should refrain from cruelty.

Spinoza does not deny that we should protect ourselves from such a person, and if he could be confused, as to what it was really sensible of him to do, by some religious or ethical superstition, it would probably be as well to inculcate him with this. The fact would remain, however, that there is no ethical truth of which such a man is showing his ignorance or disrespect in behaving as he does.

All this is said concerning a man who really would thus best preserve his own distinctive mode of being. That, however, is what Spinoza, in the end, will not allow as a real possibility. For he thinks that the kind of rationality which is really at the heart of every man means that his true satisfaction is incompatible with such conduct, which must represent an overcoming by forces alien to his true self.

This may be a trifle optimistic as a view of human nature, yet there are some considerations, of a type to which Spinoza himself appeals, which give him some support. It seems that malice, as opposed to simple animal combativeness, arises from frustration, and that it is only to the extent that a person has failed to reach the satisfactions of his most basic nature, that the pleasures of cruelty become important for him. Thus one might say that it is the man who has been defeated in his attempts to find his true good who turns to acts of cruelty, and that if he could gain a rational understanding of the frustrations which produced his cruel impulses he might see a better way of dealing with them. Spinoza also lays much stress on the need that man has for man. One might develop his own somewhat dry conception of this need by attending to what seems the very basic human need to be accepted and loved within a community, something which is hardly possible unless one finds some way of coping with cruel or malicious impulses other than by their direct indulgence.

The basic Spinozistic claim in this connection is that so far as men really understand what would satisfy them as the genuine fulfilment of their being they will behave in ways towards each other which maximize harmonious relations. It is not, of course, suggested that this means that all human conflict will be removed if people will only be just a little bit more reflective. The urges which lead to conflict are strong and difficult to resist; the point is only that on our rational side we will come to endorse habits of life and ways of organizing society which reduce the harm that these urges do.

One thing which the Spinozist thinks would reduce conflict would be a widespread recognition of the truth of determinism. Hatred and intolerance turn on thinking of other people as free causes of those actions which bring one distress of one kind or another; once one realizes that their action sprang necessarily from their nature and their situation, these emotions, the main cause of social disharmony, tend to lose their force.

It might be objected to Spinozism at this point that the same realization will presumably work equally against love. However, the Spinozist may claim that love and hate are not quite parallel here. In so far as men do evil they are victims of circumstances which do not pertain to their inner essence, while in so far as they do good their action really does spring from them. The man who is doing something constructive is expressing himself, and our enjoyment in grasping how this is so may form a kind of love for him; however, in so far as his action is merely destructive it arises from his being overpowered by forces which lie outside the core of conscious rationality which is his true self.

I cannot attempt here to give any full account of Spinoza's theory of the emotions, some of which is very illuminating, but which also suffers from certain inadequacies, as it seems to me.

All the varieties of emotion are seen as combinations formed from four basic elements, joy or pleasure as a man's passage to a greater perfection, that is a more unimpeded expression or enhancement of his essence, sorrow or pain as man's passage to a lesser perfection, desire which is the basic drive to preserve one's own distinctive form of being, and ideas of what exists in the world. Love is defined as pleasure or joy with the idea of an external cause, and hate as a similarly accompanied pain or sorrow.

Spinoza contends that hatred for fellow human beings can never be good, while love takes various forms, some of which are good and some bad. Without going into details of his argumentation on this matter, we may say that the basic theme is that the positive emotions based on that of pleasure or joy, that is on expansion of one's being, are good, except in so far as they inhibit fuller forms of such expansion, while negative emotions based on pain and sorrow are always undesirable in themselves, even if to some extent they sometimes serve to control irrational men in a socially necessary way, though it would still always be better to replace such negative motivations by more positive ones.

The basis of Spinoza's morality lies in a certain view of man's highest good and in the belief that the individual can normally only approach this good when he lives in relations of, at the least, peace with his fellows, and preferably in relations through which men contribute positively to the attainment of this good by each other through mutual example and stimulation. On this basis he establishes various principles of morality of a sort we associate with the main world religions, but differing from much Christianity, in that fulfilled living in the here and now is seen as the main objective, and in the exhortation to strengthen one's nature by meditating on one's virtues, rather than by self-abasement before an angry God.

'The man who lives according to the guidance of reason strives as much as possible to repay the hatred, anger or contempt of others towards himself with love or generosity.' Spinoza seeks to establish this and similar propositions as describing the way of life one will adopt so far as one grasps clearly what will best promote one's own personal fulfilment. Thus he does in a manner give morality an egoistic basis, deriving it from the recognition that man cannot achieve his personal good except in cooperation with others. I believe that an essentially Spinozistic position might have given a place to empathy as basic to ethics, which Spinoza does not develop, though there are pointers to it in what he does say. If one accepts that a human being cannot have a satisfactory life unless he makes an effort, crowned with some degree of success, to understand the world around him, one may then come to see that this includes under-standing the aspirations, the desires and the sufferings of other human beings, and in the end of animals too, and that this understanding of necessity brings with it concern that those desires and aspirations should be satisfied, and those sufferings checked, since as represented inside one's own consciousness they become secondary desires (and so forth) of one's own, which must be taken account of when trying to fulfil one's own primary desires. It may be suggested that, if this is so, empathy just brings fresh problems which the wise man will avoid by not developing it; however, that is to check one's own basic nisus to understanding.

Spinoza, in fact, did develop an account of 'the imitation of the affects' according to which grasping that someone has an emotion involves sharing it. Yet he seems to hold that the wise man will restrain empathy with suffering as an obstruction to his own personal self-development. It is in this spirit that he tells us that pity is evil and unprofitable when it occurs in a rational man, since it merely means that his level of perfection is reduced as well as the other man's. We should note, however, that this remark is deliberately restricted in its application to the rational man, and that this is because the rational man will recognize a more positive reason for helping others, namely the need to carry humanity with him in general in his quest for good. Spinoza makes it clear that where less rational men are concerned pity is desirable as a stimulus to the sense of human solidarity.

Perhaps there does seem something a little inhuman in the way Spinoza puts the matter. Yet it may well reflect his personal need to prevent himself from becoming engulfed by the sorrows of the world, and there is surely some wisdom in the point, later given such exaggerated prominence by Nietzsche, that those who can make something of their lives, by fortune of circumstance or nature, should not fail to do so through being overcome with commiseration for sorrows they cannot relieve. I think also there may be some confusion, on the part of Spinoza and others who have said similar things, between the pity which supplies the original motivation for the relief of sorrow, and the pity which is so persistent and pervasive that it obstructs even the actions of relief. The former supplies an essential insight into how things are, and calls forth action appropriate to its being thus, action which includes putting a check upon our own emotions.

Spinoza's basic point, in any case, is that we should seek to be motivated by positive emotions in which we see good to be achieved, and enjoy our own vitality in pursuing it, and avoid reflections which reduce our vitality. In this connection Spinoza describes techniques for dealing with our feelings which have something in common with various techniques of 'positive thinking' advocated in certain types of popularistic applied psychology of recent times, though within the context, I think, of a more realistic assessment of the human situation and of human good. Although he puts it somewhat differently, central to these techniques, I think, is the deliberate identification of oneself with whatever is constructive and positive in one's being, and a readiness to endure with what fortitude one can muster, assisted by the thought that self-blame is pointless, the negative elements of one's personality as a kind of environmental encumbrance, seeing one's victories over this, rather than one's defeats by it, as what pertains to oneself.

More needs to be said concerning that highest good of man, pursuit of which requires human cooperation and adherence to certain principles of conduct. That good is, as we have seen, each man's enhancement of his own being. Yet this characterization of it does not do justice to Spinoza's belief that it is a shared good. In seeking to bring this out, Spinoza suggests that the more fully developed we become the more we will find the focus of all our strivings in what he calls 'the intellectual love of God'.

This mysterious, to some perhaps rather off-putting, phrase has certainly been taken in somewhat different ways by different readers of Spinoza. In trying to understand it we must bear in mind that for Spinoza

God is the universe, the reality of which we are a part, not something beyond it, and that the expression 'intellectual' would seem to cover any sort of consciousness for Spinoza, so that the whole expression is perhaps equivalent to 'conscious delight in the reality we are in the midst of'.

Both this and Spinoza's own formulation may seem so general as to be vacuous. We may surmise that for Spinoza certain definite ways of experiencing the unity of the universe, and of particular things as pertaining to this unity, were denoted by the expression, but he has not managed to make it too clear to most readers what these were like, possibly because they had an ineffable mystical aspect to them.

Certainly part of what Spinoza has in mind is that one can come to know and to love the most general characteristics of the universe, and to love particular things as specifications of these most general characteristics. That might suggest that what Spinoza really recognizes as the completest form of human fulfilment is the enjoyment of the scientific researcher. Yet the truth, I think, is rather that it is the enjoyment given by any kind of understanding and discovery that he celebrates, for after all any sort of knowledge is knowledge of reality, and can be seen as a partial revelation of the general character of the universe, whether it be the physicist's knowledge of the ultimate articulation of matter, the novelist's grasp of the possibilities of human nature, or perhaps the painter's knowledge of the intrinsic possibilities of form and colour, as also the knowledge which others can gain from the productions of such people.

One thing which may mildly trouble us is that if the intellectual love of God consists in the appreciative understanding of the nature of things, the status of the enjoyment of what purports to be understanding, but is really misunderstanding, is rather unclear. After all, if Spinoza thought that at times he was loving the universe by understanding its phenomena, it is rather likely that his state was sometimes one which modern science would regard as error.

Actually Spinoza distinguishes three types of knowledge, knowledge gained by hearsay or rote learning, knowledge of an abstract kind, and knowledge consisting in an intuitive grasp of reality in the concrete, and identifies the intellectual love of God only with the third. But it is clear that what seems an example of the third may be infected with errors springing from the inadequate science which presents itself as knowledge of the second kind, so that when Spinoza thought he was in possession of the third kind of knowledge, he was very likely sometimes conceiving things in terms of scientific ideas now thought false. And surely a modern may also be the victim of falsehoods accepted as scientific truth today, while, of course, for most of us our apparent understandings very likely spring from the slightness of our grasp of any principles of scientific explanation, true or false.

It is clear enough, however, that Spinoza would claim that however much we may be in error, whenever we enjoy ourselves in working something out, or in what seems an immediate insight into how things hang together, we have in fact engaged with some aspect of the nature of reality in an understanding manner, be it only the essential structure of a certain system of concepts, this system itself being, after all, part of the nature of things. Embedded as it may well be in misunderstandings as to quite what it is to which our truth applies, misunderstandings generated outside our active thinking, that thinking itself in so far as we experience it as some kind of real achievement has certainly homed in on the true nature of some aspect of reality. I am inclined to believe that this Spinozistic claim is correct.

It does seem, however, that if the intellectual love of God means simply the enjoyment of one's own powers of thought, even if this is understood so widely as to cover any kind of conscious creative activity, it is a somewhat misleading phrase. I suspect, though, that for Spinoza it implied something of a more mystical nature, some rapturous sense of one's oneness with the cosmos at large, and of its essential oneness in all its varying phenomena.

This sense of oneness with the cosmos at large sometimes takes the form of what may be called a meditation upon pure being. One brings home to oneself the fact that everything *is*, has *being*, and directs one's consciousness to this sheer being which everything participates in having. In doing so one may realize that even what distinguishes one thing from another was always implicit in sheer being as such, inasmuch as it pertains eternally to the nature of being that the differentiating characteristics of each particular thing are among the ways in which being in general may become concrete. A Spinozist may think of consciousness and extension as built into being as such in this way, and think of every particular kind of consciousness, or type of extended thing, as a determination built into each of these as these are built into being.

There are remarks in Spinoza's *Ethics*, about the vacuousness of such a word as *being*, which appear to clash with suggestions such as these, yet I believe that in the end his intellectual love of God was, or at least included, a kind of meditation on being of this kind.

It is certain in any case that it consists in some kind of delight in

174

grasping the character of the universe, both in general and in its details, and that raises the obvious question of whether the world is not in many respects so dreadful that one can only replace love of a transcendent God by love of it through blindness either stupid or wilful.

Spinoza's answer to this question is seldom thought quite satisfactory. He says in the first place that in so far as one understands sorrows, which the course of the universe brings one's way, one's understanding of them means that the sorrow gives way to joy in one's own understanding. Thus the sorrows for which the irrational man would blame God or the Universe are for the rational man simply further joys. Likewise for any of the calamities of human kind of which one knows; they are all capable of giving the active mind the pleasure of understanding them as necessary episodes in the history of things, following of necessity from what preceded them, as that did from its predecessors, back through infinite time, in virtue of the basic and necessary features of the world considered physically or psychologically.

Here is another case where determinism plays an essential role in Spinoza's thought. The use to which he puts it here certainly seems exaggerated. Surely one neither can, nor would want to, take the atrocities of human history simply as objects one can delight in understanding and thank the universe for having provided for this purpose. Yet a somewhat modified claim may be more acceptable, namely that if they really are necessary features which the universe must possess if it is to be at all, and to possess characteristics which on balance make it good that the universe is, we may then be able to delight in the universe as a whole and in general while not denying that it has elements which are foul. Personally I believe that the only possible solution of the problem of evil, either for a more orthodox theism, or for a pantheistic position for which the universe itself is a kind of divine unity, does lie in holding that in some way, probably beyond us, everything is so bound up with everything else that the evils are essential elements in a universe to which it is still proper to take a positive attitude, and even think of as best grasped by those who love it.

Spinoza also urges that evil is in a sense unreal, appearing to be there only when we expect in one part of reality what is really only proper to another part. For example, we do not think of a cat as evil because it behaves as a cat rather than as an Albert Schweitzer in its relations with mice, and likewise we should not think of a so-called criminal as evil, and only do so because we look for qualities in him which his circumstances and nature preclude. Similarly sickness is taken as evil because we expect health, but if we simply accept each stage of life for what it is, rather than condemn it for its failure to be something else, our sense of it as evil will lapse. These remarks may shock, but I think there is more in them than at first appears, and they are not, of course, meant to suggest that we should not try to avoid the assaults of criminals and sickness. Yet though some of the evil we posit in the world does seem to arise from misplaced expectation, some aspects of evil seem more positive than this, and I suspect that Spinozism can only deal satisfactorily, if at all, with evil in the manner suggested by trying to establish that somehow it is inseparable from the being of a universe which we cannot without folly wish had never been at all.

For the Spinozist, then, this universe in which we are elements is essentially one to be loved and enjoyed; what mainly stands in the way of such love and enjoyment is mental confusion and distraction, and there are techniques for reducing these, though we have to accept that they cannot be totally eliminated. There are certainly evils which will come our way, and one must adopt an attitude of quiet endurance to these when they cannot be removed, recognizing that they are part of a scheme to be delighted in, in its totality (not as means to a greater good but as unavoidable accompaniments of what is positive in existence), while finding enjoyment in every situation in such exercise of one's own powers as it allows.

Spinozism is the most thoroughly deterministic theory of existence there is, while Sartrean existentialism is the least, yet in a curious way they often coincide. Sartre tells us we should not deceive ourselves into thinking that what we do springs from factors imposed on us from outside. Spinozism teaches us that we should be as conscious as possible of what we are about, realizing that we cannot really be forced to do anything, since (to put it thus) if we are forced it is not a doing, while if it is a doing it springs from our choice, as expression of our essence, and we should take satisfaction in our positive contribution to the situations we are in, not repine at what comes from outside us. The existentialist may think that in speaking of one's essence one tries to fob off one's actions on to a kind of internal mechanism, but this is a misunderstanding. For the Spinozist as much as for the existentialist he who repines at what he is doing is in a state of bad faith, since if it is not forced on him, and therefore not his doing, he is doing it because he wants to do it, and should adopt a joyous honesty in admitting this.

SOME RECOMMENDED READING

CHAPTER ONE: DESCARTES AND THEISTIC DUALISM

Descartes, *The Philosophical Works*, 2 vols., trans. E. S. Haldane and G. R. T. Ross, Cambridge University Press, 1911. This is still in print and contains not only the essential *Meditations* but also the important *Objections and Replies*.

Good commentaries on Descartes include:
Bernard Williams, *Descartes*, Penguin Books, 1978.
Margaret Wilson, *Descartes*, Routledge & Kegan Paul, London, 1978.
E. M. Curley, *Descartes and the Sceptics*, Basil Blackwell, Oxford, 1978.

Modern dualism of a somewhat Cartesian kind is exemplified in:
John Beloff, *The Existence of Mind*, MacGibbon & Kee, London, 1962.
H. D. Lewis, *The Elusive Mind*, George Allen & Unwin, London, 1969.
Geoffrey Madell, *The Identity of the Self*, Edinburgh University Press, 1981.

For Santayana's epiphenomenalism see:
George Santayana, *The Realm of Matter*, Constable, London, 1930.
George Santayana, *The Realm of Spirit*, Constable, London, 1940.
T.L.S. Sprigge, *Santayana, An Examination of his Philosophy*, Routledge & Kegan Paul, London, 1974.

CHAPTER TWO: MATERIALISM

Lucretius, *The Nature of the Universe*, Penguin Books, 1951.
Thomas Hobbes, *Leviathan – The First Part* (any edition).
D. M. Armstrong, *A Materialist Theory of Mind*, Routledge & Kegan Paul, London, 1968.
D. M. Armstrong, *The Nature of Mind*, Harvester Press, Sussex, 1981.

At the end of this chapter Marxism and Hegelianism are touched on. A beginner might well start with the following commentaries:
John Plamenatz, *Karl Marx's Philosophy of Man*, Clarendon Press, Oxford, 1975.
Allen Wood, *Karl Marx*, Routledge & Kegan Paul, 1981.
J. N. Findlay, *Hegel: A Re-examination*, George Allen & Unwin, London, 1969.
Charles Taylor, *Hegel*, Cambridge University Press, 1975.

CHAPTER THREE: IDEALISM

G. Berkeley, *Three Dialogues between Hylas and Philonous* (numerous editions are available).

Immanuel Kant, *Critique of Pure Reason*, trans. Kemp Smith, Macmillan, London, 1929.

F. H. Bradley, *Appearance and Reality*, Clarendon Press, Oxford, 1930.

F. H. Bradley, *Essays on Truth and Reality*, Clarendon Press, Oxford, 1968.

R. Wollheim, *F. H. Bradley*, Penguin Books, 1959.

S. S. Saxena, *Studies in the Metaphysics of Bradley*, George Allen & Unwin, London, 1967.

A. E. Taylor, *The Elements of Metaphysics*, Methuen, London, 1961.

E. Schrödinger, *My View of the World*, Cambridge University Press. 1964.

W. H. Walsh, *Metaphysics*, Hutchinson University Library, 1963.

T. L. S. Sprigge, *The Vindication of Absolute Idealism*, Edinburgh University Press, 1983.

Although he was not an idealist in a usual sense, the reader interested in exploring a theory of existence with affinities to Bradleyan idealism, but more scientifically orientated, should try the major metaphysician A. N. Whitehead. A good beginning would be *A Key to Whitehead's Process and Reality*, ed. Donald W. Sherburne, Indiana University Press, 1975, or, failing that, *Science and the Modern World* by A. N. Whitehead, Fontana Books, 1975 (first published 1926), which bears closely on the topics of the first three chapters of this present book.

The nineteenth-century American idealist Josiah Royce is very readable, and a major thinker. His many works include *The Religious Aspect of Philosophy*, *The Spirit of Modern Philosophy*, and *Lectures on Modern Idealism*.

CHAPTER FOUR: MAN AND WORLD AS WILL: THE VISION OF SCHOPENHAUER

Arthur Schopenhauer, *The World as Will and Representation*, Dover Publications, New York, 1966. The older translation of this work as *The World as Will and Idea*, trans. R. B. Haldane and J. Kemp, Routledge & Kegan Paul, London, 1948, is less accurate but adequate.

Patrick Gardiner, *Schopenhauer*, Penguin Books, 1963.

Michael Fox (ed.), *Schopenhauer: His Philosophical Achievement*, Harvester Press, Sussex, 1980.

D. W. Hamlyn, *Schopenhauer*, Routledge, & Kegan Paul, London, 1980.

Bryan Magee, *The Philosophy of Schopenhauer*, Oxford University Press, 1983.

CHAPTER FIVE: NIETZSCHE AND THE WILL TO POWER

Works by Friedrich Nietzsche:

Thus Spoke Zarathustra, translations by W. Kaufmann in *The Portable Nietzsche*, ed. W. Kaufmann, Chatto & Windus, London, 1971, and by R. J. Hollingdale in Penguin Classics, 1961.

Beyond Good and Evil, trans. R. J. Hollingdale, Penguin Books, 1973.

On the Genealogy of Morals, trans. W. Kaufmann and R. J. Hollingdale, Vintage Books, New York, 1969.

Twilight of the Idols, translations by W. Kaufmann in *The Portable Nietzsche* and by R. S. Hollingdale in Penguin Classics, 1968.

The AntiChrist, translations as for *Twilight*, the Hollingdale translation in the same Penguin Classic volume.

The Will to Power, trans. W. Kaufmann and R. J. Hollingdale, Vintage Books, New York, 1968.

The numerous books on Nietzsche in English include:

Walter Kaufmann, *Nietzsche, Philosopher, Psychologist, Antichrist*, Vintage Books, New York, 1968.

R. J. Hollingdale, *Nietzsche: The Man and His Philosophy*, Routledge & Kegan Paul, London, 1973.

Bernd Magnus, *Nietzsche's Existential Imperative*, Indiana University Press, 1978.

CHAPTER SIX: HEIDEGGER AND BEING-THERE

Martin Heidegger, *Being and Time*, trans. Macquarrie and Robinson, Basil Blackwell, Oxford, 1973.

Martin Heidegger, *An Introduction to Metaphysics*, trans. Manheim, Yale University Press, 1959.

Martin Heidegger: Basic Writings, ed. D. F. Krell, Routledge & Kegan Paul, London, 1978. (This volume is recommended as providing the best way in to the study of Heidegger.)

Joseph P. Fell, *Heidegger and Sartre*, Columbia University Press, 1979.

W. B. Macomber, *The Anatomy of Disillusion*, Northwestern University Press, 1967.

CHAPTER SEVEN: SARTREAN EXISTENTIALISM

Works by Jean-Paul Sartre:

The Transcendence of the Ego, trans. Williams and Kirkpatrick, Noonday Press, New York, 1957.

The Psychology of Imagination (translator unnamed), Methuen, London, 1972.

Sketch for a Theory of the Emotions, trans. P. Mairet, Methuen, London, 1962.

Being and Nothingness, trans. Hazel E. Barnes, Methuen, London, 1957.

Existentialism and Humanism, trans. P. Mairet, Methuen, London, 1977.

Critique of Dialectical Reason, trans. Sheridan-Smith, Verso, London, 1976.

The many books on Sartre in English include:

Peter Caws, *Sartre*, Routledge & Kegan Paul, London, 1979.

Istvan Mezsaros, *The Work of Sartre, Volume 1: Search for Freedom*, Harvester Press, Sussex, 1979.

CHAPTER EIGHT: SPINOZISTIC PANTHEISM

Spinoza, *Ethics*. Until a new translation, by E. M. Curley, appears, it is best to use translations based on the one by W. Hale White. Volumes including such are *Spinoza: Selections*, ed. J. D. Wild, Charles Scribner's Sons, New York, 1930. and *Ethnics* by Spinoza, ed. J. Gutman, Hafner Press, New York, 1949.

H. H. Joachim, *A Study of the Ethics of Spinoza*, Clarendon Press, Oxford, 1901.

Stuart Hampshire, *Spinoza*, Penguin Books, 1951.

Errol Harris, *Salvation from Despair: A Reappraisal of Spinoza's Philosophy*, Martinus Nijhoff, The Hague, 1973.

Marjorie Grene (ed.), *Spinoza: A Collection of Critical Essays*, Anchor Books. New York, 1973.

E. M. Curley, *Spinoza's Metaphysics*, Harvard University Press, 1969. (This last work, among the most important recent studies, is an advanced treatment of Spinoza's metaphysics, and does not deal with his moral outlook.)

The book by myself cited under Chapter Three (page 178) aims to synthesize idealism and Spinozism.

CHRONOLOGY

Some readers may appreciate having the following list of dates of first publication of the original or classic statements of the theories of existence discussed in this book.

Lucretius	*On the Nature of the Universe*	55 B.C.
Descartes	*Meditations on First Philosophy*	1641
Hobbes	*Leviathan*	1651
Spinoza	*Ethics*	1677
Berkeley	*A Treatise concerning the Principles of Human Knowledge*	1710
	Three Dialogues between Hylas and Philonous	1713
Kant	*Critique of Pure Reason*	1781
Schopenhauer	*The World as Will and Representation*	1819
Nietzsche	The works recommended above (page 178) appeared between 1883 and 1895 (except *The Will to Power* which was published posthumously)	
Bradley	*Appearance and Reality*	1893
Heidegger	*Being and Time*	1927
Sartre	*Being and Nothingness*	1943
Armstrong	*A Materialist Theory of the Mind*	1968

INDEX

MORE ABOUT PENGUINS, PELICANS,
PEREGRINES AND PUFFINS

For further information about books available from Penguins please write to Dept EP, Penguin Books Ltd, Harmondsworth, Middlesex UB7 0DA.

In the U.S.A.: For a complete list of books available from Penguins in the United States write to Dept DG, Penguin Books, 299 Murray Hill Parkway, East Rutherford, New Jersey 07073.

In Canada: For a complete list of books available from Penguins in Canada write to Penguin Books Canada Limited, 2801 John Street, Markham, Ontario L3R 1B4.

In Australia: For a complete list of books available from Penguins in Australia write to the Marketing Department, Penguin Books Australia Ltd, P.O. Box 257, Ringwood, Victoria 3134.

In New Zealand: For a complete list of books available from Penguins in New Zealand write to the Marketing Department, Penguin Books (N.Z.) Ltd, Private Bag, Takapuna, Auckland 9.

In India: For a complete list of books available from Penguins in India write to Penguin Overseas Ltd, 706 Eros Apartments, 56 Nehru Place, New Delhi 110019.

THE PROBLEM OF KNOWLEDGE
A. J. Ayer

What is knowledge, and how do we *know* things? Moreover, how do we know that we know them, in view of the doubts that the philosophic sceptic casts on our grasp of facts? The presentation of the sceptic's arguments leads here to a general discussion of the topic of scepticism and certainty. This is followed by a detailed examination of the philosophical problems of perception, memory, and our knowledge of other minds, which occupies the greater part of the book. In the course of the discussion Professor A. J. Ayer has also attempted to throw light upon the nature of the philosophical method and upon some of the problems connected with time, causality, and personal identity.

VIOLENCE FOR EQUALITY
Inquiries into Political Philosophy
Ted Honderich

Is political violence justifiable?

With force and elegant reasoning, Ted Honderich questions the morality of political violence and challenges the presuppositions, inconsistencies and prejudices of liberal-democratic thinking.

For this volume, the author has revised and greatly enlarged his highly praised *Three Essays on Political Violence*. The five essays which go to make up *Violence for Equality*, given as political philosophy lectures in Britain, Ireland, the United States, Canada, France, Africa and Holland, in fact comprise a completed treatise on the subject.

PHILOSOPHY AS IT IS
Edited by Ted Honderich and Myles Burnyeat

Ted Honderich and Myles Burnyeat set out to fulfil four aims: to represent philosophy as it is; to represent it through clear, non-technical essays; to represent recent developments in philosophy; to give the reader in an introduction to each essay an admirably lucid resumé of its arguments. Where the essays become difficult the editors say so, but in most cases the general reader will find that, among others, Bernard Williams on Utilitarianism and moral integrity, Richard Wollheim on art as a form of life, A. J. Ayer on perception and the physical world, Donald Davidson on mental events, Saul Kripke on identity and necessity and Alvin Plantinga on God, freedom and evil, offer a welcome, but not insuperable, challenge.

PHILOSOPHY THROUGH ITS PAST
Edited and Introduced by Ted Honderich

The central concerns of the great philosophers – from Plato to Wittgenstein – explored and interpreted by the greatest philosophers of our day.

From Gregory Vlastos on 'Plato: The Individual as an Object of Love', to Arthur Danto on 'Sartre: Shame, or, The Problem of Other Minds', this book explores the central concerns of the past masters of philosophy. It extends across a whole spectrum of approaches: some essays lean towards the historical, seeking truth as much as possible in the thought of the great master, while others are more inclined to suppose that philosophy advances, so that attention to the past must be selective, and certainly judgemental. All of them however, illuminate the vital past of philosophy, for the issues discussed are not only perplexing and challenging, but very much alive.